D1001555

WITHOUT LOVE

By PHILIP BARRY

Plays

THE YOUNGEST

YOU AND I

IN A GARDEN

WHITE WINGS

JOHN

PARIS BOUND

HOLIDAY

HOTEL UNIVERSE

TOMORROW AND TOMORROW

THE ANIMAL KINGDOM

THE JOYOUS SEASON

BRIGHT STAR

HERE COME THE CLOWNS

THE PHILADELPHIA STORY

LIBERTY JONES

WITHOUT LOVE

Novel

WAR IN HEAVEN

Without Love

A COMEDY IN THREE ACTS

By

PHILIP BARRY

COWARD-McCANN, INC.

NEW YORK

TO DANA WINSLOW ATCHLEY

WITHOUT LOVE *was first presented by The Theatre Guild at the St. James Theatre in New York City on November 10, 1942. It was directed by Robert B. Sinclair, the incidental music was composed by Richard E. Myers, and the setting was designed by Robert Edmond Jones. The featured players were Katharine Hepburn and Elliott Nugent.*

CHARACTERS

PATRICK JAMIESON
QUENTIN LADD
MARTHA LADD
JAMIE COE ROWAN
KITTY TRIMBLE
PAUL CARREL
PETER BAILLIE
RICHARD HOOD
EMMET RIORDAN
GRANT VINCENT
ANNA

ACTION AND SCENE

The play takes place in the course of two years in the living-room of the late Senator James Owen Coe's house in Washington. The Scenes are as follows:

ACT I

Scene 1: Late afternoon, May 9th, 1940.
Scene 2: Early the following morning.
Scene 3: Afternoon, ten days later.

ACT II

Scene 1: Early April, early evening, 1941.
Scene 2: Night, the following June.

ACT III

Scene 1: Evening, early October, 1941.
Scene 2: Night, late November, the same year.

WITHOUT LOVE

ACT I

ACT I

*The Living-room of the late Senator
James Owen Coe's house in Washington
is a long, spacious, high-ceilinged room.
The proportions are good but the decora-
tion and furnishings are in the sedate,
rather heavy Senatorial tradition of a
wealthy public servant kept in semi-perma-
nent office by a loyal New England con-
stituency. It is a house that befits a station,
but although the Living-room makes this
point in every detail, the final effect is, on
the whole, sobering rather than forbidding.
The entrance is through double doors and
down a pair of shallow steps from the main
hall at Left. Opposite it, to the right of an
imposing fireplace, a single door leads into
the Library, an even more solemn room,
lined with the late Senator's lawbooks and
political trophies and presided over by a
few busts of the Great of Antiquity.*

*The heavy, well-built sofas and chairs of
the Living-room are relieved somewhat
by summer slip-covers of natural-colored
self-striped linen. The oil paintings and en-*

3

gravings on the panelled walls are covered with crisp tarleton. In the back wall three rather small windows look out across a terrace down a wooded slope to one of the many gullies of Rock Creek Park.

It is late afternoon on the 9th day of May, 1940. The room is brighter on summer afternoons than at other times and at present a sombre and agreeable glow pervades it. Half reclining against a pile of pillows on a sofa, droopily resplendent in morningcoat, linen waistcoat, spats, ascot and wilted gardenia, is QUENTIN LADD. *He is thirty and of an athletic build which is just beginning to show symptoms of the inevitable corpulence which will one day be his. Above the broad shoulders, the wellshaped head presents a face which is genially handsome even in sleep—as now. At the piano, softly playing* "Slumber on, my Little Gypsy Sweetheart," *is* PATRICK JAMIESON. *He is a year or two older than* QUENTIN, *but looking that much younger. He is slightly built and somewhat less formally attired in a dark blue suit, white shirt and dark tie. His face, intensely awake, can be described neither as handsome nor genial. Although attractive in expression and regular enough in feature,*

*there is too much awareness, too sharp a
humor in the eyes and around the mouth,
too lean, too keen a look for his and, at
times, other people's comfort. He is
watching his companion with patient,
somewhat critical amusement. Finally he
stops playing and speaks:*

PAT:

Still sleepy?

He waits a moment, then inquires further.

Still sloppy?

Waits again and then concludes:

Still somewhat of both, it seems.

*There is another silence. He rises from
the piano, finds a cigarette, lights it, and
continues:*

American weddings are wonderful things. It's a
long time since I've attended one, a long time since
I have seen the grim, the inevitable Fall of the House
of Usher.—Well, slumber on, my little tipsy sweetheart.

ANNA, *a middle-aged housemaid, comes
into the Hall doorway.*

ANNA:

Shall I bring it in here as soon as it's ready?

PAT:

Will you do that, please?

She turns and goes out. PAT *continues to*
QUENTIN.

5

Your car's out front when you come to. It's low on gas. Goodbye. Good luck.

> QUENTIN *mumbles something inarticulate.*
> PAT *inquires:*

What's that you said?

QUENTIN:

Better check the oil too.

PAT:

She'll take two quarts.

QUENTIN:

Throw it in.

> PAT *makes a low sound like a police siren. Then:*

PAT:

Pull over to the curb, you!

QUENTIN:

Wha' for?

> PAT *stands over him, speaking softly.*

PAT:

You heard me, brother.

QUENTIN:

> *Mumbling.*

I donno where it is. *What* fire?

PAT:

You see this gun?

> QUENTIN *gestures vaguely.*

QUENTIN:

Put it away. My name's Quen—Quentin Ladd. I

6

contribute annually to the Nassau County Fund for—

> PAT *picks up a book from the table, opens it and slams it shut.* QUENTIN *leaps up from the sofa.*

Why, you—!

> *He blinks, steadies himself and stares around him.*

Where am I? What time is it?

> PAT *looks at his watch.*

PAT:

Twenty to seven, Wednesday, May 9, Anno Domini 1940.

> *He consults the back of an envelope.*

And you are at Twenty-twenty-four Rock Creek Drive, North West. The "North West" told me it was Washington. Are you willing?

QUENTIN:

How'd I get here?

PAT:

I drove you down from Baltimore. You remember Pop Emerson's wedding? Terrapin and champagne? Oh, lots of champagne!

QUENTIN:

Never take the stuff—disagrees with me. Scotch, I take, and now and then a tray of cocktails.—Then where's *my* car?

PAT:

Outside. I drove you down in it.

7

QUENTIN *eyes him suspiciously and reseats himself.*

QUENTIN:

Thanks very much, I'm sure.

PAT:

Not at all. They brought it to the door for you and you started to step in and missed—so I picked you up and brushed you off and put you in and brought you home.

QUENTIN:

Home?—I don't live here! This is my cousin's—Jamie Rowan's.

PAT:

Is he expected in? Because it's time I—

QUENTIN:

It's a she.

PAT:

"Jamie"?

QUENTIN:

Named after her old man, the late Senator.

PAT:

"Rowan"?

QUENTIN:

James Owen Coe, from the State of Maine. Rowan's her married name. She doesn't live here, either—just comes in from Virginny now and then when my Dad or I—

PAT:

Nice little pied-à-terre.

8

QUENTIN:

—Come down to talk things over with her.—Yes.
Cute, isn't it?—Rugged comfort.

PAT:

I wish it were mine. It would make a wonderful
base for operations.

QUENTIN:

What's your line, stranger?

PAT:

I'm a reformed economist just out of Europe—with
a sudden new sense of human relations.

QUENTIN:

I don't get you.

PAT:

You will. So will others, I hope.
He looks around him.
I don't suppose your cousin would care to lend her
house for a worthy cause?

QUENTIN:

She might. She's a funny sort of dame.

PAT:

How funny?

QUENTIN:

She's hardly cracked a smile in years.

PAT:

Money's a wonderful thing to keep the face
straight.

9

QUENTIN:

She lives alone, walks alone, rides alone—she even eats alone!

PAT:

Sounds pretty dismal.

QUENTIN:

Is very. Stick around and meet her. She's an experience. She and my wife will be—
> *Suddenly his face clouds.*

My God! Martha!

PAT:

Be of good heart. Daisies won't tell.

QUENTIN:

What about a drink—if there *is* one in the place?

PAT:

One's coming.

QUENTIN:

Good man.
> *He accepts a cigarette from* PAT.

Oh, thanks. It's weddings that really get me down.

PAT:

Why them, especially?

QUENTIN:

I get to thinking of my own. My home life's—er— I'm not a very happy man—er—Jamieson, did you say your name was?

PAT:

That's right.

QUENTIN:

You married, Jamieson?

PAT:

No.

QUENTIN:

Never?

PAT:

Not once.

QUENTIN:

You're lucky.

PAT:

I don't always think so.

QUENTIN:

Take it from me, Jamieson, you're lucky.

PAT:

All right, Q. Ladd, I'll take it from you and I'll put it in my pipe and smoke it.—Now, if you don't mind, I have to—to blow.

QUENTIN:

No, no—don't go yet.

PAT:

"To blow." God bless American slang—always new —especially after fourteen years away from it.

QUENTIN:

Stick around. You said you would.

PAT:

But you're O.K. now. My function is fulfilled.

QUENTIN:

Don't go. I'd be lonely. I might even do some harm to myself.

PAT:

I've got to find *my*self a hotel—small, convenient, cozy, cheap.

QUENTIN:

Hard up?

PAT:

Not terribly. But I do need to keep the overhead down.

QUENTIN:

I know a place called The Anchorage—Q Street and Connecticut Avenue. I'll drive you down there as soon as I check with Martha.

PAT:

Thanks: a very friendly act indeed.

QUENTIN:

What actually are you up to here?

PAT:

In Washington?

QUENTIN:

Such a dump.

PAT:

It seemed a good place to start doing my bit— though what bit it's to be, I'm blessed if I know yet.

QUENTIN:

You think we'll be dragged into this phony war?

PAT:

I think we'll be blasted in, and I don't think Poland
and Norway are phony.

QUENTIN:

You're an odd kind of guy, aren't you?

PAT:

Very—in fact, exceedingly. Also I'm a desperate guy
because I've been scared.

QUENTIN:

By what?

PAT:

Fourteen years of Europe—and now one week—just
one—of America.—Oh, brother, brother—if you
knew what you're in for here!

QUENTIN:

You're kidding.

PAT:

Not me. Not any more.

QUENTIN:

But you can't seriously mean you want a govern-
ment job?

PAT:

Not a job—*the* job—the one for me—the one I'll be
best at. I'll find it, if it exists—and if it doesn't I
expect I'll just have to create it.

QUENTIN:

This place is a sink hole: you go down it and never
come up again.

PAT:

Not me: it's my dish. For the first time in my life I think I know what I'm about, and where I belong: just doing Jamieson's Bit—do you mind?

QUENTIN:

Honestly, you burn me up.

PAT:

That's a nice expression, too. What does it mean?

ANNA *comes in with a tall glass on a tray.*

Here's your drink.

QUENTIN:

I can use it.—It means you slay me.—Lord, it's black! This will knock me for a—what is it?

ANNA:

Iced coffee, sir. The gentleman ordered it for you.

QUENTIN:

Isn't there any liquor in the house?

ANNA *nods primly.*

ANNA:

—But Mrs. Rowan always keeps the keys.

PAT:

It seems to me that Mrs. R. could stand a little shaking down—or could she?

ANNA:

Excuse me, sir?

QUENTIN:

What time did she say she'd be back?

ANNA:

She didn't.—I think she and Mrs. Ladd just went

14

to do some shopping, and to interview servants. The agency telephoned they were sending a man here for her to see.

QUENTIN:

A man?

ANNA:

A caretaker, they said, so I suppose it's for here.

QUENTIN:

Did Mrs. Ladd leave any message for me?

ANNA:

Just to say that you and she would be dining out. Mrs. Rowan will have a tray in her room as usual.

QUENTIN:

Thanks. That's fine.

> ANNA *goes out.* QUENTIN *stares into his glass.*

Dining out: I can't face it.

PAT:

Then why don't you tell her so?

QUENTIN:

It wouldn't do any good.

PAT:

Is it true that the women really rule here? Is that part of what's the matter, maybe?

QUENTIN:

No maybe about it. Oh, why did I ever get married again?

PAT:

Again?

QUENTIN:

Twice. Two solid times. Am I crazy?

PAT:

Well, why did you?

QUENTIN:

The same old story: I fell in love again.

PAT:

You do pick the flimsiest of pretexts here.

> MARTHA'S *voice is heard from the Hall.*

MARTHA:

Anna, be an angel and take this upstairs.
> QUENTIN *rises.*

QUENTIN:

Martha? Is that you?
> *And turns again to* PAT.

I want you to meet my wife—wonderful girl,
Martha.
> MARTHA *comes in. She is twenty-four,*
> *smart and pretty and discontented.*

MARTHA:

What a miserable, hot afternoon. Why anybody
who doesn't have to, lives in this wretched town is
beyond my—
> *She sees* PAT.

Oh—

QUENTIN:

Er—my wife—Mr. Jamieson, dear.

16

MARTHA:

How do you do.

PAT:

How do you do.

MARTHA:

I suppose you were on the wedding, too?

PAT:

Yes, I was there. I knew the groom.

MARTHA:

> *To* QUENTIN.

How was it—the usual?

QUENTIN:

Just about. Where's Jamie?

MARTHA:

She'll be in. There was something about a caretaker coming. Honestly, I simply can't talk to the girl any more. She gets odder and silenter each time I see her.—What on earth are you drinking?

QUENTIN:

You'd be surprised.

> *He holds the glass out to her. She sniffs disdainfully at it.*

MARTHA:

Coffee! What imaginable idea is there in drinking foul black coffee at this time of—?

> *Then, significantly.*

Oh—I *see.*

QUENTIN:

Do you? That's fine.

> *He drains the glass.* MARTHA *proceeds to lash herself into a fury.*

MARTHA:

You "overdid" it again, as you say, didn't you?—Why in the name of heaven, it seems to be utterly impossible for you to appear at the simplest gathering without getting yourself into a completely drunken state, is something beyond me. I know you're not exactly a Great Brain, but really, Quentin—

QUENTIN:

Look, Martha, behave, will you?

MARTHA:

How? What am I supposed to do—cheer wildly whenever you make a spectacle of yourself? Will you kindly get dressed? We're dining with the Parkers.—And without imbibing further, if you please!

> QUENTIN *smiles foolishly.*

QUENTIN:

Not even a little cock of the tail that bit me?

> PAT *laughs.* MARTHA *turns on him.*

MARTHA:

So you think that's funny?

> *Suddenly* PAT *is very serious.*

PAT:

Why yes, moderately.

18

MARTHA:

Well, *I* don't!

To QUENTIN.

I think you're simply obscene. Jamie will be pleased too, won't she? Naturally she won't say anything, but she'll know.

She glances scornfully at PAT.

—You and your drinking companions.

PAT:

After a moment.

Why, you disagreeable little piece, you.

MARTHA:

I beg your pardon?

PAT:

It's a long time since I've seen one of you on your home court. Is it the lime in the soil or something? You ought to have your mouth washed out with soap, you spoiled little witch.

MARTHA:

What do you think you're saying?

PAT:

Exactly what's in my mind to say! How dare you humiliate this sweet fellow before an absolute stranger?

MARTHA:

Well! Who do you think *you* are?

PAT:

I know quite well who I am. What interests me, is

19

what conceivable training you can be the product of.

MARTHA:

Quent—who *is* this man? I've never been talked to so in my life.

PAT:

Then it's high time someone began.

MARTHA:

Quentin!

QUENTIN:

Easy there, boy.

PAT:

Take her upstairs and lock her in her room.

QUENTIN:

Now look here, Jamieson—

MARTHA moves swiftly toward the Hall.

MARTHA:

Quentin! Get rid of that man and come this minute.

She goes out. QUENTIN hesitates a moment, then:

QUENTIN:

Would you care to step outside with me?

PAT:

Don't be a priceless idiot.

He gestures toward the Hall.

Go and consolidate your position.

QUENTIN:

My—what do you mean?

PAT:

Listen—I usually charge for unpleasant work like this—

QUENTIN:

I get you.

PAT:

Then go on—follow through.

> QUENTIN *goes out.* PAT *takes a deep breath, picks up his coat from the chair, puts it over his arm, picks up his hat and stands there. He glances around himself at the room and shakes his head over it.* JAMIE ROWAN *comes silently in, behind him, from the Hall. She is 27, expensively but unbecomingly dressed, pale and rather dim looking. Her features are good, but nothing has been made of them. She seems to be an object, rather than a person. In appearance, in voice, in manner there is an apparent lack of personal awareness. She stops and glances disinterestedly at* PAT'S *back, then advances toward him. She speaks mechanically but at the same time effortlessly.*

JAMIE:

Good afternoon.

> PAT *turns and looks at her.*

PAT:

Good afternoon.

> *She studies him a moment. Then:*

JAMIE:

I'm afraid you won't do.

PAT:

No?

JAMIE:

No. I wanted an older man.

PAT:

> *After a moment.*

I'm older than I look.—I thought you'd be older, too.

JAMIE:

What has that to do with it?

PAT:

I beg pardon, Madam.

JAMIE:

What is your name?

PAT:

Patrick Jamieson.

JAMIE:

Irish, I presume?

PAT:

By descent, Ma'am: all four grandparents. For myself, I'm an American citizen, as was my father before me.

JAMIE:

Are you single?

PAT:

Very much so.

JAMIE:

That's also unfortunate: I wanted a couple. Something in the nature of superior caretakers for this place, which I intend to offer for sale—furnished—just as it is.

PAT:

I am sure I could show it to the greatest possible advantage.

JAMIE:

I'm afraid it would be too lonely for one person alone. I'm sorry.

PAT:

I'm a great reader, Madam.

JAMIE:

As it happens, there's quite a large library. Still, I'm afraid that wouldn't—

PAT:

And could I maybe play the piano?

JAMIE:

Why, of course I should have no objection to that, if—do you play the piano?

PAT:

Quite well—and there's no better company for a lonely man anywhere.

23

JAMIE:

My father used to play the piano for hours on end. He—

She stops herself.

But that's quite beside the point. The fact is—

PAT:

—He must have been a great man, the Senator.

She ponders a moment. Then:

JAMIE:

Perhaps if I could get someone in by the day to cook for you—

PAT:

That would do it.

He places his hat and coat on a chair.

JAMIE:

May I see your last references—er—what is it you like to be called?

PAT:

How do you mean?

JAMIE:

"Patrick" or "Jamieson"?

PAT:

Whichever comes easiest.

JAMIE:

There'd be an afternoon off once a week—and every evening unless I particularly wanted you to be here.

PAT:

You could ring me up.

JAMIE:

And—how much are you asking—if I may ask?

PAT:

In this case, lodging and meals would be quite enough. I don't think I could stand to have money pass between us.

JAMIE:

You would have wages suitable to the position, Patrick. Whether or not you would be suitable for it, I'm not yet sure.—The references, please?

> *He pats the pockets of his jacket, frowning.*

PAT:

The fact is, I've got none. I expect you'd just have to take me on faith, Jamie.

JAMIE:

But naturally I could not—

> *Her voice slows, her eyes widen. She rises abruptly.*

What did you say?

PAT:

I said you'd have to take me on faith—

> *He waits an instant, then smiles and adds:*

—Jamie.

JAMIE:

Good afternoon.

PAT:

Honestly, you burn me up.

> *She presses a button beside the fireplace.*

25

JAMIE:

Will you leave at once, please? I should have known better than to—

> QUENTIN *comes in from the Hall.*

—Quentin, will you please see to it that this—this insolent—

QUENTIN:

Hello, James—how are you?

> *He bears down on* PAT *and throws an arm around his shoulder.*

And my wonder boy—my prince among men! You're God's gift to husbands.—Jamie, this man is Aces. He's our next President.

JAMIE:

Will you kindly explain to me what on earth—?

> PAT *bows and gestures toward* QUENTIN.

PAT:

My references, Madam.

> MARTHA *comes in and up to* PAT.

MARTHA:

Mr. Jamieson, I want to thank you for what you did for my husband after the wedding. It was terribly nice of you.

PAT:

It was a pleasure.

MARTHA:

Now are you sorry you spoke so rudely to me?

PAT:

Not a bit. It did you good.

MARTHA:

You fiend.

ANNA *enters.*

JAMIE:

You absolute—!

ANNA:

Please, Madam.

JAMIE:

Yes, Anna?

ANNA:

A man is here from the Atlas Agency.

JAMIE:

After a moment.

Will you tell him I'm sorry, but the position is filled?

PAT:

Wait a minute! You know I was only—

JAMIE:

You presented yourself for the place, did you not?

PAT:

But naturally it was just for the fun of it.

JAMIE:

You stated your terms?

PAT:

Well—yes. But a joke's a—

JAMIE:

They were met, were they not?

PAT:

Yes, I'll have to admit that you—

JAMIE:

Then I'm afraid we shall have to consider it binding.
>> *To* ANNA.

Please say I'm sorry, I've already engaged a man.

ANNA:

Very good, Madam.
>> *She goes out.* PAT *laughs.*

PAT:

All right—one on me.

JAMIE:

Ha. Ha.

PAT:

And one on you maybe!—I think it's going to be very nice for me here. Of course you may want to consult your husband about it.

JAMIE:

My husband is no longer living.—You and Quentin are dining out, Martha?

QUENTIN:

Not me.

MARTHA:

But I told them!

QUENTIN:

Telephone.

MARTHA:

But at this hour, what can I—?

QUENTIN:

Just tell them politely I'm drunk in a gutter.

MARTHA:

This is the limit, Quent.

She storms out again.

This is about all I need. If this isn't mental cruelty, I don't know what is!

JAMIE:

Why don't you all have dinner with me?

QUENTIN *stares at her, unbelieving.*

QUENTIN:

Together? You mean it?

JAMIE:

Yes. I'd love it if you would.

QUENTIN:

Is there enough in the house for the four of us?

JAMIE:

If there isn't there easily can be. Oh, please say you will!

PAT:

We will.—Lord, that terrace is really something—and what an evening! How do you get to it?

JAMIE:

There's a door from the dining-room.

PAT:

There ought to be another here. Couldn't we kick one through and dine out there?

JAMIE:

Why, I suppose we could. I hadn't thought of that.

ANNA *comes in.*

Will you set a little table for four on the terrace, Anna?

ANNA:

On the terrace, Madam?

JAMIE:

Yes, Anna, on the terrace.

> ANNA *goes out.* PAT *goes to* JAMIE.

PAT:

And may I have the keys to the wine closet, Madam?

JAMIE:

To the—?

PAT:

Yes, Madam, to the wine closet.

> JAMIE *goes to the desk, finds a bunch of keys.*

JAMIE:

It's the brass one. I don't know how long it is since it's been used.

PAT:

It's a shame to have to keep a lovely thing like wine locked up. You might be a shade more trustful.

> *She gives him the keys.*

JAMIE:

Anna will show you.

PAT:

I think you may be a girl who has kept a lot of

precious things locked up for many precious years.—
Thank you, Madam. You slay me.

> *He tosses the keys into the air, catches*
> *them again and goes out, whistling gaily.*

QUENTIN:

Mad, I don't think. Odd, I grants ye.—Look, James:
Father wanted me to get your reaction on shifting
out of some low-yield Governments into the Pre-
ferreds of certain war industries that would stand
to benefit, if—

JAMIE:

Quentin—tell me one of your funny stories. I want
to laugh some more.

Curtain

ACT I

SCENE 2

*The Scene is the same. The room is dimly
lit by a single lamp and by the gradually
increasing light from outside, it being
about six o'clock the following morning.*
PAT, *in dressing-gown, trousers, slippers, is
seated at the piano playing, very softly. He
finishes, waits a moment, staring at the
keys, then closes the piano and leans forward, his head on his arms upon it, one
hand rising and falling limply on its cover.*
JAMIE *comes in quietly from the Hall. She
is in pajamas, slippers, a dressing-gown.
For a moment she stands on the step in
the Hallway, looking down at his bowed
head without speaking. When at last she
does, it is in a very low voice:*

JAMIE:

Is that all you are going to play?

PAT:

That's all.

JAMIE:

It's been truly lovely.

Slowly PAT *raises his head and gazes at
her.*

PAT:

You? Where did *you* come from?

JAMIE:

I've been sitting on the stairs, listening, for an hour.—I play a little too, but nothing like as well as you do.

PAT:

Perhaps you'd like to take over?

She comes down into the room.

JAMIE:

No thanks. Thanks very much, but no thanks.

PAT:

I'm terribly sorry if I woke you up. I thought the house was big enough—that you were far enough away—

JAMIE:

You didn't wake me. I was awake.

PAT:

Do you have it too?

JAMIE:

It?

PAT *gestures.*

PAT:

Can't sleep—insomnia.

JAMIE:

Sometimes.—But it must be six o'clock now—after six.

PAT:

I hope I didn't disturb anyone else.

33

JAMIE:

I'm sure you didn't.—All the time, do you have it?

PAT:

A good deal of it.

JAMIE:

You said a number of astonishing things after dinner. Have you always had this—prophetic sense?

PAT:

It's not that. It's more of a kind of a new time-
sense I've grown. But it doesn't always work. For
instance, I was telling them in Paris just one month
ago that by April fifteenth at the latest the Germans would—and here it is well into May and still
no further move.—Look: just because *I* can't sleep,
there's no reason why you—

JAMIE:

I'm going to stay right here. I know what it's like
to be wakeful, with no one to—

> PAT *moves away from her restlessly.*

PAT:

Then talk—just talk, will you? Talk my ear off.

JAMIE:

What about?

PAT:

Yourself. That's always interesting.

JAMIE:

Not *my* self.

PAT:

Suppose you let me be the judge of that. Go on—

trot it out! Where'd you come from? Whither bound? I like to know all about people.

JAMIE:

>*After a moment.*

I was born in Nineteen hundred and fourteen in the New England town where my father was born, and his father before him—my mother, too.—Is that the way?

PAT:

That's it—keep going.

JAMIE:

We lived in a big brick house—bigger than this and, like this, with no reason for it. I was the only child and even I didn't appear till several years after Father and Mother married. I guess he knew I was all he was going to get and that's why he named me Jamie. Mother never was very strong but I remember that she was terribly sweet and really quite pretty—

PAT:

I can believe it.

JAMIE:

She died when I was eight and it was then that Father first went into politics—to try to forget her, I expect. He was good at them, as he was at most things, and when he got to be governor he was the youngest one there'd ever been in the State of Maine.

35

PAT:

Why's it always the *State* of Maine? Why not just—

JAMIE:

Because it's so big and so wonderful I expect. Father loved me dearly and I simply worshipped the ground he walked on. We were together every spare moment he had. I rode with him and shot with him, we even went on fishing-trips together, when I was old enough. Mrs. Prentice, the housekeeper, was nice, but not very communicative; she was a true native, if there ever was one. Miss Jennings, my governess, I always secretly hated, and I hate her now. She made me terribly shy with people and frightened the life out of me about God and Purity.

PAT:

You probably had a good healthy reaction.

JAMIE:

No. The fact is I never did. By Gum, I'm still scared. I pray for guidance and I blush when I get it. I didn't go to boarding school till I was fifteen, and only for two years then, because Father was elected Senator and wanted me here in Washington with him.

PAT:

How long was he Senator?

JAMIE:

Till he died, six—nearly seven years ago—December 1933, it was.

36

PAT:

When did you marry?

JAMIE:

Earlier that same year—in June.—I know how to make coffee.—Would you like some coffee?

PAT:

No—let's wait. You haven't finished.

JAMIE:

Anna might be up—I know she gets up awfully early.

PAT:

Where did you meet him—your husband? What was he like?

JAMIE:

She's a Catholic and in town she likes to go to early Mass. I'll—

PAT:

—Why don't you want to talk about it? Wasn't it a happy marriage?

JAMIE:

It was a very happy marriage.

PAT:

Then—

She smiles at him uncertainly.

JAMIE:

You might tell me something about yourself first, don't you think? You seemed most noncommittal after dinner—even about the "Jamieson's Bit" you're here to do. After all, if you're going to live in my house without references—

PAT:

I was born six years before you were, in Elgin, Illinois, where my father practiced law before he got hipped on the Foreign Service. He was a brilliant, most lovable, honest, erratic man. When I was eighteen he was made Minister to Ireland and that was grand; we loved it. There was that lovely house in Phoenix Park and I went to the University of Dublin. Father got on famously with the Irish and so did I. Ireland— Good Lord, how Britain needs her —Lord, how we're going to! But how to get them to bury that old hatchet?

JAMIE:

Is that maybe what Jamieson's Bit is to be?
He glances at her sharply.

PAT:

Holy Hat, if it could be!

JAMIE:

Yes—but in the meantime keep a-going about you.

PAT:

Later I studied for awhile under Keynes in London and then I began to do my stuff. Father was with Biddle in Warsaw and I was there analyzing the cock-eyed commerce of a once partitioned country for King Features, when the invasion came. Father and I manned an ambulance together. It was day and night work and he caught pneumonia and died very quickly. I was on the last train out of Poland—finally got to Paris, where something else happened that also shook me up pretty badly—

He hesitates and stops.

JAMIE:

What was that?—I'm sorry. Of course, if you don't want to say—

PAT:

I don't know why not—it was a girl. She got married.—Lila Vine. Lila the beautiful, Lila, the true Belle Dame sans Merci. She was the Europe I loved, American though she was.

JAMIE:

What was she like? I mean—

PAT:

She was bright and gay and shallow and lived for parties. She was forever humming or singing magical French songs and saying, "What, Darling? What, Sweet?"—It was a thoroughly devastating, supremely joyless affair.

JAMIE:

Couldn't it have been otherwise?

PAT:

No, because she had no heart. I tell you this caddishly and honestly: she was a witch on a broomstick. She wouldn't have me and she wouldn't let me go. The last time I saw her she was wearing a white evening dress with her curls piled on the top

39

of her head, looking about sixteen—oh—what the hell!

JAMIE:

I think most girls have a white dress they remember, or are remembered in. And of course if one falls in love in one—

PAT:

Love! You can have it—anyone who wants it can. Not for me—no, Madam, never no more. I've had enough of that sickness, thank you.

JAMIE:

Don't call it that!

PAT:

That's what it was for me—and believe me, if I ever felt the slightest symptoms of it again, I'd show its fair object the cleanest pair of heels ever a girl saw.

JAMIE:

It's odd, this—it's very odd.

PAT:

What is?

JAMIE:

You never want love in your life again, I never want it in mine. But our reasons are as different as the sun is from the moon.

PAT:

Yes. I grant you that's odd.

JAMIE:

You don't want it because you had all the worst of it. I don't want it because I had all the best.

PAT:

Was it like that?

JAMIE *inclines her head.*

JAMIE:

—His name was—his name *is* Harry Rowan. He was twenty-two when we met. I was twenty. He was just getting out of the University of Virginia, where Father went to make the Commencement address. We were in love before we knew it, deeply and instantly. We were married in a month and went to live on the sweet farm his grandfather had left him —White Gate, where I live still—and we set to work to raise prize cattle and breed thoroughbred horses. He was the finest, the kindest, the gentlest human being I have ever known. He had a first-rate mind and was very amusing. I was amusing then, too—or he seemed to think so. We laughed a great deal together, we were so young and everything was such great fun.

PAT:

He must have been something, all right.

JAMIE:

He was everything. For two years it was heaven on earth, every living, breathing moment of it, perfection.

PAT:

Only two years?

JAMIE:

That's all—but it was a lifetime, really. Then one

morning early—a morning just like any other one
—he went out with the Middleburg Hounds on a
green hunter. It seems that he behaved all right at
first and then without warning suddenly refused a
fence—and threw Harry, marvelous rider that he
was. He landed the wrong way, the terribly wrong
way, as sometimes happens, even to the best. They
brought him back to me and he lived long enough
to—to grin his grin at me and say, "What a dirty
trick on us, Jamie, but don't think we end here."

> *She gestures slightly.*

So you see—

PAT:

Yes. I think I do.

JAMIE:

And do you beg my pardon?

PAT:

I beg your pardon.

JAMIE:

Thank you.

> *For a moment they do not speak. Then*
> *she gestures again.*

There. Now you have my whole story—the simple
one of a simple girl who wants no more of life because life has no more to give her.

PAT:

You should not say that.

JAMIE:

I say it, however—and mean it, believe me.

PAT:

I know you do, but it's wrong. It's a complete denial of life. You can't close the books on life just where and when you choose. That's not allowed.

JAMIE:

No? By whom is it not?

PAT:

I'm not quite sure. By the heavenly powers, I expect—and the hellish ones.

JAMIE:

Both to the contrary, I shall do as I wish.

PAT:

But it's so stupid. It's such a waste! In these, of all days, to be in possession of a rudimentary brain and a powerful commodity like money, and make no real use of it: It's shocking to me. It's profoundly shocking.

JAMIE:

Have you any suggestions?

PAT:

Certainly! Use it to wake people up to what's coming. Use it for horses for new Paul Reveres! One if by land—two if by sea—three if by air! Give it to China—give it to The Committee for Defending—! But no—I forget—that's not how the rich stay rich.

JAMIE:

Are you trying to be vulgar?

PAT:

It's no effort. Never anyone expect the little gentleman of me again. I was that long enough. There are plenty of them in England and in France, very deft at volcano dancing. And from what you've said of him, I doubt if Harry Rowan was any such as they.

JAMIE:

Why?—If it hadn't happened what do you think he would be doing now?

PAT:

Getting ready—and getting others ready!

JAMIE:

He—had a way of seeing ahead, too.

PAT:

It's a pity his horse hadn't.

> *Her shoulders contract sharply. He glances at her and adds:*

I did that deliberately.

JAMIE:

Yes. I know you did.

PAT:

One derives a certain satisfaction at times from seeing how much a person can take.

> JAMIE *looks at him long and intently.*

JAMIE:

You fancy yourself as being as hard as nails, don't you?

PAT:

Not quite, but it's time to toughen up—and past time.

> *He bows to her, mockingly.*

44

—With my kindest regards to the rich and idle, Madam, for their delicate graces.

PAT:

And with mine to all such as you for your acquired pride—your overbearing manner—your lack of taste!

PAT:

Shall I go?

JAMIE:

Will you please?

PAT:

Of course. On the dot.

> *He moves toward the Hall. He slows, and stops at the steps, turning to her.*

—Also a satisfaction to know there's still a spark of life left in you.

JAMIE.

Thank you so much.

PAT:

Not at all.

JAMIE:

—And goodbye.

> *He chuckles. She demands:*

What's that for, may I ask?

PAT:

I was just thinking that being wakeful with a girl can be almost as good as—

JAMIE:

—Well, you needn't!

45

PAT:

I forgot about New England.

> *He smiles and half salutes her.*

Farewell from the Middle West—

> *And turns again to the Hall.*

—Via Europe.

JAMIE:

Please don't go.

> *He returns to her, faces her. She speaks in a low voice.*

You've seen it, haven't you?—you, with your eyes.

PAT:

Maybe—but what?

JAMIE:

My loneliness.

PAT:

I thought—but I wasn't sure.

> *She holds out a hand to him.*

JAMIE:

Will you take my hand?

> *He takes it, gazes at it. She looks up again, smiling uncertainly.*

And will you stay and be my friend?

PAT:

If you like. People need them in this kind of world. But I'm not an easy one.

JAMIE:

I know—and I don't want you easy. Is it a go?

46

PAT:

Anyway, it's a try.

JAMIE:

It would be good to have a friend.

PAT:

It would be good to have a pretty girl to—to be
wakeful with.—I'll take a quick shave and a tub.
Breakfast?

JAMIE:

By the time you're down.

> QUENTIN *comes in from the Hall with the*
> Washington Post *in hand. He raises his*
> *brows at them.*

QUENTIN:

What's this, what's this!

JAMIE:

Hello, Quentin. What got you up this early?

QUENTIN:

I couldn't stay down. I thought I heard music. I've
never had that before.

> *He opens the paper and scans the head-*
> *lines.* PAT *moves toward the Hall.*

PAT:

That's very bad. The next stage is—

QUENTIN:

—Holy cats!

JAMIE:

What is it, Quent?

47

QUENTIN:

Look here—

She glances at the headlines.

JAMIE:

Pat!

PAT:

What?

JAMIE:

Your time-sense wasn't so far off as you thought, my friend.

He moves swiftly to them, gazes at the paper spread open in QUENTIN's *hands.*

PAT:

God, oh God!—Yes, this does it, all right! There she goes, boys—the joke's over.

QUENTIN:

—Right smack into the Low Countries on high. Nothing phony about this, I'll admit.

PAT:

There'll be lots to admit in the next few weeks, brother.

QUENTIN:

Sort of gives a fellow a start, doesn't it?

PAT:

I hope so. Boy, I hope!

The THREE *stand in a group, silently, intently reading the news.*

Curtain

ACT I

SCENE 3

The same, about ten days later, a little after three o'clock in the afternoon. The Living-room is as before except for the removal of some of the bric-a-brac, the tasseled piano-cover, and the addition of a few vases of flowers. It being earlier in the day than in Scene 1, there is more light from outside. The entire effect is considerably less crowded and more cheerful, although there is still a long way to go.

The Library door is opened from within and KITTY TRIMBLE *enters, followed by* PAT. KITTY *is about twenty-six, small, slim and pretty. She looks capable and very much her own man, which she is. She gazes about her at the room.*

PAT:

The drawing-room—living-room—wherever you want to call it. Which completes the tour. Unless perhaps you'd like to see the cellar?

KITTY:

The cellar I shall take on faith. I'm sure it is capacious, sound, impregnable to damp and full of rats.

PAT:

No bodies, however.

KITTY:

Not even of political enemies?

PAT:

I can vouch for the absence of bodies, Miss Trimble. If you want bodies, you will have to go elsewhere.

KITTY:

I gather the library's *your* special nook.

PAT:

I even sleep there at times.

KITTY:

It looked it. What's your subject or subjects?

PAT:

History—Human Beings—Ant Life generally.

KITTY:

But look, Mr. Jamieson—just who are you, and what is your function here?

PAT:

Friend of Mrs. Rowan's and Keeper of the Keys.

KITTY:

Would she lease for a term of years or must it be an outright sale?

PAT:

She wants to sell.

KITTY:

You know what she'll get for it? Two cents.

PAT:

I'm sure she won't consider anything less than

three. Of course I haven't seen her for a week or so—she may have changed her mind.

KITTY:

What time is she due in from the country?

PAT:

Any time now.

KITTY:

I told my clients we'd meet here at five.

PAT:

Your "clients." Then you *are* a real estate agent.

KITTY:

No kidding—honestly not. Phooey on real estate agents—my partner and I wouldn't stoop.

PAT:

A partner, too, eh?—Then what *do* you call yourselves?

KITTY:

"Contacts, Incorporated." We fulfill a very useful function. "Contacts" knows the ropes, knows the people, knows the places: whom to see, where to go for it, how to swing it. It provides backgrounds, foregrounds and middle-grounds—chiefly middle: it is a master of the art of collaboration and compromise—but it isn't doing very well.

PAT:

Well, I asked!

KITTY:

Do you happen to need a good secretary? I'm serious. Or do you know anyone who does?

PAT:

I'll be thinking.

KITTY:

Full or part time. A lady must live.

PAT:

Even if it's by her wits: I quite agree.

KITTY:

—Unless, of course, she's got money.

PAT:

Even with money, wits and more wits! The one thing you can't live on in these times is your own fat, whether it's in your head or your heart or just on your ribs.

KITTY:

I haven't a great deal on my ribs.

PAT:

I noticed that.

KITTY:

And I don't think there's any at all in my head. I have a rather stout little heart, however.

PAT:

Who or what does it tick for?

KITTY:

Its owner, chiefly.

PAT:

That would have been my guess.

KITTY:

Still, there are occasions—when one's not too busy—

PAT:

I'll make a note. What's your slack season?

KITTY:

Late spring—any time now.

PAT:

Shall we say dinner at The Carlton tonight at eight o'clock?

KITTY:

That would be lovely—but are you that rich?

PAT:

No, nowhere near it.

KITTY:

Then here—

She fumbles in her handbag for a card.

On my card. It's a darling place and the food's good—and also I get rates there.

PAT:

It's a date.

KITTY:

You know, you're a sort of a curious number, even for this town. Are you anybody?

PAT:

Not yet.

KITTY:

All the same, you seem to know where you're going —which is rare, hereabouts. Could Baby help on the way?

PAT:

Baby might. What are your fees?

KITTY:

Surprisingly low, for the services rendered.

PAT:

It would have to be on a deferred-payment basis.

KITTY:

Acceptable, when our interest is engaged.

PAT:

You're a good girl, Miss T.

KITTY:

No—please don't make that mistake.

PAT:

Which one?

KITTY:

The "good girl." I'm quite a bad little girl—and I revel in it. Does that shock you?

PAT:

As a matter of fact, it does, somewhat.

> *He gazes at her. She inquires coolly:*

KITTY:

Well—what do you see?

PAT:

One of the damnedest creatures I've ever run into.

KITTY:

So do I. So we'll either fight like wolves, or get on famously. The prospect pleaseth—

> JAMIE *comes into the Hall doorway.*

JAMIE:

Hello, Pat!

> *She sees* KITTY.

54

—Oh—hello, Pat.

PAT:

Hello, Jamie. It's nice to see you again.

JAMIE:

It's been ages, hasn't it?

PAT:

It's been all of that. This is Miss Trimble—Mrs. Rowan.

KITTY:

How do you do.

JAMIE:

How do you do.

PAT:

Miss Trimble came about the house.

JAMIE:

Oh, yes?

PAT:

She's not a principal, nor is she exactly an agent. But whatever she is, she revels in it.

> KITTY *gives* JAMIE *a card. She reads it and laughs.*

JAMIE:

"Contacts"—what an enchanting name.

KITTY:

Provocative, don't you think?

JAMIE:

Extremely. Those two men prowling in the garden belong to you, then?

KITTY:

I'm afraid they're my clients—and the White House car because Peter Baillie is one of them.

JAMIE:

I see.

PAT:

Baillie? Isn't that one of the President's new right-hand men?

KITTY:

That's right. But naturally the house isn't for him. He's bringing someone from—what's the name of that foreign news agency?

PAT:

Reuter's?

KITTY:

No—the French one.—Anyway, he's after a house for some bigwig who's coming for the Purchasing Commission.

PAT:

There'll be plenty of them from now on, I expect.

KITTY:

Yes, I shouldn't be surprised.

> *To* JAMIE.

—But it's only to rent.

JAMIE:

I wanted to sell it.

KITTY:

Awfully few are buying, now. You see, if the Administration changes next Fall—

PAT:

Don't worry; it won't.—I'd hold on to the house if I were you, Jamie. With a little thought and doing over—for instance, that door to the terrace—it could be charming. Sell when the boom comes, if sell you must.

JAMIE:

I'll have to think about renting, and let you know.

> ANNA *comes in from Hall with two cards on a tray.*

KITTY:

But of course. I quite understand.

ANNA:

A Mr. Baillie and a Mr. Carrel to see you, Madam.

JAMIE:

Please ask them to come in.

ANNA:

Very good, Madam.

> *She goes out.*

PAT:

Baillie's supposed to have a bit on the ball, isn't he?

KITTY:

He certainly is.—But what you have on the ball is "a lot," not "a bit."

PAT:

"A lot on the ball." "A lot on the ball."

> *Again* ANNA *comes into the doorway.*

ANNA:

Mr. Peter Baillie. Mr. Paul Carrel.

57

> *And goes out again as* PETER BAILLIE *enters. He is about fifty, small, slight, nervous, intense. He looks ill and tired, but the keenness is there and instantly apparent.* PAUL CARREL *is in his early forties, tall, distinguished, handsome.* KITTY *advances.*

KITTY:

Mr. Baillie? I'm Kitty Trimble.

PETER:

Of course. I remember.

> *He takes her hand.*

Contact!

KITTY:

Mrs. Rowan—may I present—?

JAMIE:

How do you do, Mr. Baillie.

PETER:

Greetings and so forth.—Mr. Paul Carrel, Mrs. Rowan. Mr. Carrel is foreign correspondent for the Agence Havas: French equivalent of the A.P. or U.P.—We get 'em too.

JAMIE:

How do you do?

> CARREL *advances and kisses her hand.*

CARREL:

Enchanté, Mademoiselle.

JAMIE:

But I'm afraid it's "*Madame*."

CARREL:

Pas possible!

JAMIE:

But it is.—And my friend Mr. Jamieson—Mr. Baillie.

PAT:

How are you, Mr. Baillie.

PETER:

I'm all right. And you? Good!

PAT:

Paul—

CARREL:

Pat Jamieson! Not since Geneva!—What are you here for?

PAT:

Oh—just to stir up more trouble in a shaken, shattered world.

PETER:

"Jamieson"—that's the name of a whisky.

PAT:

Irish—and a good one. That is, if you can take it.

PETER:

I can take it.

PAT:

Yes—I understand you have a lot on the ball.

> *To* CARREL.

How are all the girls? Remember Denise?

CARREL:

And do you remember Lila?

> *He turns to* JAMIE, *gazes at her intently.*

But I find this one very charming—more American than was Lila.

PAT:

Careful, Jamie—he's a regular rakehell.

JAMIE:

Really? How nice. I don't think I've ever met one.

CARREL:

Do you like white violets?

JAMIE:

If they're fresh—but I'm sure that any from you would be.

PETER:

I thought this was about a house.

CARREL:

I think your house is ridiculous.

JAMIE:

You what?

CARREL:

Absurd—fantastic—the American equal of my grandmother's at Neuilly—which I have loved with a love since my boyhood.

JAMIE:

You—mean you like it, then?

CARREL:

I adore it. But now Mr. Baillie is taking me to meet your President. We cannot be late—so may I examine it in detail another time?

JAMIE:

Whenever you wish.

60

CARREL:

That will be soon.—When will you lunch with me, Pat?

PAT:

I can't lunch. I'm working too hard.

PETER:

Here? At what?

PAT:

Oh, just my bit—just the little job I believe I can do well. We've most of us got one of those, don't you think?

PETER:

Individualist, eh?

PAT:

Till it's time to take orders.

>   *To* CARREL.

Some day for a drink, though, Paul.

CARREL:

Will you ring me up?

PAT:

Right.

CARREL:

Mademoiselle—à bientôt.—Miss Trimble, a word if you please—

>   *He moves toward the Hall.* KITTY *follows him.*

KITTY:

>   *To* PAT.

I like purple ones.

PAT:

I'll try to remember.

> CARREL *and* KITTY *go out.* JAMIE *turns away, frowning, preoccupied.* PETER *is still watching* PAT.

PETER:

"Jamieson."—Was your old man by any chance the Jamieson in the Foreign Service?

PAT:

By every chance.

PETER:

He was something too, that one.

PAT:

Yes, I agree with you.

PETER:

Great job in—Ireland, wasn't it?

PAT:

Among other places.—Do you know Ireland?

PETER:

No—can't say I do.

PAT:

Cute little spot—wonderful for an invasion: no Maginot Line, no Siegfried, no Mannerheim: just hedgerows and cozy unfortified ports.

PETER:

So?

PAT:

—So. Funny thing: Napoleon said that if he'd have

gone into it instead of to Egypt, he'd have had England cold in a month.

PETER:

So?

PAT:

—So. People must read more.
A brief pause. Still PETER *studies him.*

PETER:

How'd you like to come along with us now and say Hello to the Boss?

PAT:

No, thanks—thanks very much, but no, thanks. I'm not interested in just saying "Hello" to him. I've got too much to talk to him about. Perhaps sometime when he could manage a couple of hours—

PETER:

A couple of—! Are you sure that will be enough?

PAT:

At first—and any time it's convenient, of course. I've no dates I can't break.

PETER:

That's fine. Goodbye, Mrs. Rowan. Thanks.

JAMIE:

Thank you for coming in. Come again.
She rings for ANNA.

PAT:

Do you like to get letters?

PETER:

Why?

63

PAT:

Because I'd like to send you a weekly one on certain current aspects of the British Isles. Is that all right?

PETER:

Oh, certainly! Anything else?

> PAT *moves toward the Hall with him.*

PAT:

I hope you're none of you counting too heavily on the French.

PETER:

Not if you say not to.

PAT:

I suppose, if the letters interest you, you might bring one or two to the President's notice?

PETER:

Oh, of course—I could hardly fail to do that!

> ANNA *appears in the Hall.* PETER *follows her out.* PAT *speaks lowly:*

PAT:

Jamieson takes his bit in his teeth.

> *He moves to* JAMIE. *Suddenly she seems to shiver.*

What's the matter, Jamie?

JAMIE:

That man had the oddest effect on me.

PAT:

Baillie? *I* thought he—

JAMIE:

No—the other—the Frenchman.

64

PAT:

—And don't think he didn't intend to have.

JAMIE:

Him and his white violets!

She turns and smiles at him.

How are you?

PAT:

Fine.

JAMIE:

Have you been sleeping?

PAT:

Not too much.

JAMIE:

Thanks for your accounts of the people who came to the house.

PAT:

I thought you were entitled to regular written reports.

JAMIE:

They were fun. I enjoyed them. They made me laugh. I was afraid you'd be bored, just—being here this way.

PAT:

Hell, no: I've been documenting myself like a house afire.—But you—you look different somehow. What have you been up to all this time?

JAMIE:

Nothing much.—Just riding about forty miles a day

65

—not hunting—not to get anywhere—just around by myself—just riding and thinking.

Now she is being very off-hand.

PAT:

Big thoughts?

JAMIE:

Enormous ones.

PAT:

What about?

JAMIE:

Oh—Life with a great big "L."

PAT:

That's sometimes rewarding. How did it come out with you?

JAMIE:

Not very well.

PAT:

Anything I can do about it?

JAMIE:

There might be.

Then, after a moment.

To tell the truth, that's why I came in this afternoon.

PAT:

Really?

JAMIE:

Yes, really!

66

PAT:

Tell me what I can do, Jamie. There's nothing I could that I wouldn't.

JAMIE:

Why isn't there?

PAT:

Because I *like* you with such a great big "L." Will that do?

JAMIE:

Do you truly? Are you sure you do?

PAT:

No. I'm just imagining it.

JAMIE:

In a rush.

That's nice—because I've been imagining that I like you a good deal too. And we're so utterly different that we *could* help each other, couldn't we?—I mean really help. That is, if we—if we—

PAT:

If we what?

JAMIE:

Don't rush me. Give me time.

PAT:

One, two, three, four—

JAMIE:

—You see, it's as I told you: I've been thinking all sorts of things and in all sorts of ways—backwards, forwards, every which way—but chiefly forwards.

PAT:

I hope that means you've stopped settling for the past.

JAMIE *nods eagerly.*

JAMIE:

Yes! Yes—that's it.—And I got to thinking maybe you're right. Maybe the whole world *is* going to tremble and shake and shatter around us—and maybe all we live by and for *is* truly threatened—and that's an awful world to live in alone—and a terrible time to go through by oneself.—And—and you've got such qualities to face it with—to do something about it with—your eye is so clear—you see so straight—you're so honest, so quick, so—aware of everything —and fearless and forthright and—

PAT:

Madam! Wait a minute—

JAMIE:

No! Don't stop me now!—And—and though I'm none of those things, except maybe honest, I've got qualities for it, too. I—I'm strong and have lots of energy—and I'm brave too, in a way: things don't get me down—and I can take punishment—and if it *is* all to be that way, with such great things at stake, I want to be—I must be part of it! I can't just stay outside—nobody any good can. But I—I just don't want to be all alone through it. I want someone to lean on a little—yes, and to stand by, as well! I can do that!

68

PAT:

I'll bet you can.

JAMIE:

—So I thought that after all we said to each other that first night—and the way we understand each other a—about love and so forth—I mean really— you know how *I* never could and I know how you never could or would or would want to—and there's all that—you know—what you call "that powerful commodity" to be put to use—and so I thought—

PAT:

Thought what?

JAMIE:

—So you see, I wondered if maybe you'd like to marry me. Would the idea interest you?—Because, by Gum, I'd like you to!—Because all of a sudden I've seen that there may be another basis for a good and happy marriage, besides love.

PAT:

And what is it, would you say?

JAMIE:

—Several of them: things shared in common—hon-esty, say and courage and and humor?—Though I haven't got much of that, I'm afraid.

PAT:

I think you have—I think you're full of it, or you'd never have thought up anything like this.

JAMIE:

It *is* sort of funny, isn't it?

PAT:

It's hilarious.

JAMIE:

Then why don't we laugh?

PAT:

Because it just wouldn't work.

JAMIE:

Why not? Because of—because of ghosts?

PAT:

Because of lots of things.

JAMIE:

If you're interested at all, I demand that you think it over!

PAT:

Jamie, you fool, you're out of your head.

JAMIE:

I'm not—I'm into it! It's you who's the fool for not seeing the—the possibilities.

PAT:

Two people—Americans both—marrying without love on either side?—With no hope of it—no desire for it, even?

JAMIE:

But that's just it! I could never even think of it, if someone loved me. I'd feel so guilty all the time. And you—you certainly wouldn't want someone mooning over you, would you?

PAT:

No—I can't say I would: no time: much too busy.

JAMIE:

And those two Americans—those special two—
they'd have other things, wouldn't they? They'd
have understanding—and companionship—and the
independence you prize so. And they'd be safe forever from the other side of love—the side you said
you knew.

PAT:

I knew it, all right: the exacting, the demanding
side. The jealousy—the possessiveness—the misery—
the general hell.

JAMIE:

There'd be none of that—there couldn't be.

PAT:

It would present a nice little problem in human
relations, I'll grant you that.

JAMIE:

Drive out to the country with me—have dinner and
spend the night! Old Auntie Bess is there, so you
won't be compromised. We'll talk everything out
from the beginning to—

PAT:

—Dinner tonight? The—damn it—the trouble is, I've
made an engagement. But maybe I could—the trouble is, it's with a girl.

JAMIE:

Then keep it, by all means.—See how unpossessive I
am? We'll talk here. Or we'll just forget the whole
thing.—I feel as if I'd run a mile.

PAT:

I wonder if we really might make a go of it.

JAMIE:

What have we to lose, Pat?

PAT:

For each other's sake we'd have to present ourselves awfully well: get perfectly and exactly into step and stay there.

JAMIE:

I realize that: publicly, we'd have to seem—well—unusually devoted.

PAT:

That wouldn't be hard, Jamie—even privately.

JAMIE:

I know it wouldn't be for me.—One thing though, Pat: I—I don't believe I could ever again sleep in the same room with a man.

PAT:

Don't worry.—I wouldn't share a room with anyone, if I could avoid it. Anyhow, I think the importance of sex in marriage is very much overrated.

JAMIE:

It would have to be in this one.—I mean to say—

PAT:

You'd never have to give it a thought, Madam.

> *He finds* KITTY's *card and goes to the telephone with it.*

Deference—preference: a very good rhyme.

72

JAMIE:

White Gate is lovely, really it is.

PAT:

We'll decide which to swing on—it or each other.
>   *She rises abruptly,* as *he dials the telephone.*

JAMIE:

What's that?—Pat, what *is* it?

PAT:

Shut up, my sweet innocent.

JAMIE:

If it's what I think it is, I simply won't allow it!

PAT:

How are you going to help yourself?
>   *She tries to take the telephone from him.*

Hello? Contacts, Inc.?

JAMIE:

Stop it, please! We can go out tomorrow just as well. Honestly, I—

PAT:

—Is Miss Trimble there? No? Well, will you take a message for her, please?

JAMIE:

Pat—I tell you there's really not the slightest need to—!

PAT:

Will you tell her that Mr.—
>   *To* JAMIE.

—What's my name?

JAMIE:

Jamieson.

PAT:

—That Mr. Jamieson called—J-a-m-i-e-s-o-n—to say that he has made a contact that makes dinner to-night impossible and can she change it to tomorrow or Wednesday instead? In fact, you'd better say lunch on Thursday—

He covers the mouthpiece and looks to JAMIE.

Do I get Thursday off this week?

JAMIE:

If you're a good boy.

PAT:

To the telephone.

Thursday at one at the same place, if I'm a good boy.—Got it? Contact! Thanks. Goodbye.

He replaces it and returns to her.

JAMIE:

Secretly, I'm very pleased. It's very pleasant to be preferred.

PAT *kisses her cheek. She kisses his.*

PAT:

"Jamie Jamieson"—it would be quite a pretty name.

JAMIE:

Don't *think* I didn't think of *that!*

Curtain

WITHOUT LOVE

ACT II

ACT II

The Living-room has undergone a number of changes. The position of the furniture has been changed, some of the pieces replaced with less heavy ones, and the linen slip-covers removed. Most of the bric-a-brac is gone. The few remaining paintings are good, and are free now of the tarleton coverings. Lamps, or certainly lamp-shades, are different. The floor is almost entirely covered with a fine old Aubusson, handsome in pattern and warm in color. The most striking change in the room, however, is the large bow-window which has been built out from the back wall, to replace the original small windows and to give access through French doors to the terrace. These doors are now open and a portion of the brightly furnished and awninged terrace may be seen, and beyond it a small grove of silver birches rising from the ravine in the Park. There are a number of vases of summer flowers about and the room is still brightly lighted with the afternoon sunlight. It might be a different

77

*room in a different house, but one sees that
it has merely undergone a complete and
becoming transformation. It is about six
o'clock of an afternoon in early April
the following year, which is to say, April,
1941.* KITTY *is busy at the desk with bills
and a check-book. The telephone rings beside her. She answers it.*

KITTY:

Hello? Who?—Oh yes—yes, of course.—In the
morning? About ten? Here or at the Legation?—
Yes, I'm sure Mr. Jamieson will be delighted to see
him then. Thank you. I'll put it down.

*She replaces the telephone and makes a
note.* QUENTIN *comes in from the Hall.*

QUENTIN:

Hello.

KITTY:

Hello, yourself.

QUENTIN:

Why? What's wrong?

KITTY:

Nothing except that I hate household accounts.
How long are you here for?

QUENTIN:

Just a couple of days. Been months, hasn't it? How
are the newlyweds?

78

KITTY:

Hardly newly no more, but fine, fit and fettle-some.

QUENTIN:

No patter of tiny feet as yet?

KITTY:

I haven't been listening.

QUENTIN:

It's well over the yardarm. I ordered a cocktail or two.

KITTY:

Good for you—also me.

QUENTIN:

Where are they? Pat and James, I mean?

KITTY:

She's out for tea. He's still in there, plugging. I've been kicked out again.

QUENTIN:

Look here, Kitty—I call you Kitty, don't I?

KITTY:

I don't know. It's been so long, I forget.

QUENTIN:

Look here, Babe: what's it all about?

KITTY:

All what?

QUENTIN:

All this razzle-dazzle of Pat's—this English-Irish whatnot.

KITTY:

It's not razzle-dazzle, nor is it yet whatnot.

QUENTIN:

Then what is it?

> ANNA *comes in with a tray and three Martinis.*

KITTY:

Can't say. I'm a confidential Sec. Here's your Mart.
Drink up.

> *She takes one.*

Thank you, Anna—

> QUENTIN *takes the others.*

QUENTIN:

Thanks twofold.

> ANNA *goes out.*

ANNA:

They'll do you no good.

QUENTIN:

It's harm I like done me.

> *He downs one at a gulp.*

—Are you using your contacts for him?

KITTY:

Not one. He won't let me. He's strictly on his own.
Contacts Inc. is no more.

QUENTIN:

—Before we even made one.

KITTY:

Leave us brush away a furtive tear.

> *She blinks at him unconvincingly.*

QUENTIN:

Don't do that, or I'll make two bites of you.—Seriously—how long since you've been kissed?

KITTY:

Seriously? Let's see, now—what's today? Last night, I guess.

QUENTIN:

When would you like to be again?

KITTY:

I think I'll wait till after my cocktail, if that's all right with you.

QUENTIN:

I can last, I guess. Look: I've about decided that armed intervention is not definitely impossible.

KITTY:

No?

QUENTIN:

Yes. And I know all about boats and I fly my own plane. Why shouldn't I get into Naval Aviation on the ground floor, and land a commission?

KITTY:

I'd slip you one in a minute.

QUENTIN:

A fellow gets sort of bored with being just a—an immature sportsman.

KITTY:

Ladd, you're truly beguiling. I like you.

QUENTIN:

Then why don't you finish your cocktail?

KITTY:

There—it's gone.

QUENTIN:

Stand up—

She does so.

—And tilt your head back a little. I'll be right with you.

He downs his other drink. KITTY *raises her face.*

KITTY:

Like this, Lieutenant?

QUENTIN:

Smart girl: you got it straight off.

He moves to her, leans and kisses her.

How's that?

KITTY:

Very good, Commander. How's for a return engagement?

QUENTIN:

H.M.S. "Dauntless," three points off the starboard bow.

She kisses him, is soundly kissed in return, then stands in his arms, her cheek against his chest. She exclaims softly:

KITTY:

Admiral! That was a Destroyer—

QUENTIN:

Us Naval Aviation Desk-Job Men—who can resist us?

82

KITTY:

Head her for home again, Sailor.

> *Again she raises her face, but stiffens suddenly as she sees* JAMIE *coming in from the Hall in a pretty and becoming afternoon dress, with a bunch of white violets tucked in the belt.* KITTY *abruptly leaves* QUENTIN'S *arms.*

QUENTIN:

Hey! What happened?

> *Then he sees* JAMIE *too, smiles foolishly and explains.*

—I was just receiving my commission.

JAMIE:

Please go on with it—it's such a pretty ceremony.

QUENTIN:

Where's Martha?

JAMIE:

She went up to dress.

QUENTIN:

I'd better do the same.

JAMIE:

One minute, Quent.

> *She tidies his face with his own handkerchief and replaces it in his pocket.*

There! Now you're decent again. In fact, you look cherubic.

QUENTIN:

Thanks.—In fact, I feel it.

He turns and waves as he goes out.

See you some more, Kitty!

JAMIE *regards* KITTY *accusingly.*

JAMIE:

Why, Miss Trimble—aren't you ashamed!

KITTY:

Don't you go trying to make me feel guilty, now.

JAMIE *laughs.*

JAMIE:

Kitty! I wouldn't dream of it. It looked such fun.

KITTY:

It often is.

JAMIE:

Often? Does it really happen to you often?

KITTY:

No more so than is good for me.

JAMIE:

It just never does to me.

KITTY:

Well, I should hope not.

JAMIE:

Why?

KITTY:

You're different.

JAMIE:

How?

KITTY:

From me? Well, you're a person of some stature.

84

JAMIE:

"Stature"?—You mean tall? I'm not so tall.

KITTY:

I mean tall in soul.—In addition to which, you're married.

JAMIE:

In addition to which, I'm from New England.

KITTY:

So you see?

JAMIE:

Oh dear—

KITTY:

You can't seriously mean that you want passes made at you.

JAMIE:

No—I'd just like to feel that someone might want to.—Of course there *was* that Brazilian who tried to hold hands under the table, but I expect that was just being neighborly.—And do you live with men too, Kitty?

KITTY *looks somewhat startled.*

KITTY:

Look here—what's all this sudden preoccupation with—?

JAMIE:

—I'm just curious to know. I wouldn't ever tell.

KITTY:

I'm not promiscuous, if that's what you mean. I may have been slightly so at one time, but not now.

85

JAMIE:

It must be strange to be a mistress. I don't think I'd know quite how to act.—But rather pleasant, maybe. Don't you ever feel conscience-struck?

KITTY:

No, I can't say I do.

JAMIE:

You're so wonderfully—worldly, I guess it is.

KITTY:

You're not so bad.

JAMIE:

But I couldn't be the mistress even of a situation.

Then, thoughtfully:

Except maybe I was today. I just may have been.

KITTY:

How do you mean?

JAMIE:

You know who I had tea with?—Paul Carrel, at his flat.

KITTY:

Not alone!

JAMIE:

Oh yes, all-a. Just me and Paul, Paul and me.

KITTY:

Jamie! What on earth would induce—?

JAMIE:

I found out he'd found out what Pat is doing: you know—playing both ends against the middle, as he calls it.

86

KITTY:

He's not going to do a story on him! He's not going to spill all our beautiful beans at *this* point!

JAMIE:

Oh Kitty, I hope not! I hope I persuaded him how unfair it would be.

KITTY *nods cynically.*

KITTY:

Sure—all he needed was some emotional female, preferably a wife, to clinch the truth of a few rumors for him.

JAMIE:

You don't understand. That's just what I wasn't.

KITTY:

Wasn't what?

JAMIE:

Emotional. I was cool and collected as ever could be. That's the point of me, Kitty—*I'm* a special sort of wife.

KITTY:

A—?

JAMIE:

It's a secret formula.

KITTY:

But what did Paul *say?* What did he agree to?

JAMIE:

He said he'd have to think about it and let me know: professional ethics or something involved.

KITTY:

—The usual. Well, Mr. Jamieson's present jig's up, I guess.

JAMIE:

But I don't think so! I really believe I convinced him that—

> PAT *comes in from the library.* KITTY *speaks lowly:*

KITTY:

Are you going to tell him?

JAMIE:

Not about this. But there's something else I— Hello, Pat!

PAT:

Mr. Jamieson is tired. Mr. Jamieson would like a drink. How are you, fellows?

> JAMIE *goes to make a drink for him.*

KITTY:

Oh, just dandy.

PAT:

Jamie, my girl?

JAMIE:

I'm not sure. I feel light and wiley and obscure.

PAT:

What does that mean?

JAMIE:

I don't know.

88

PAT:

We've been going out too much with too many furriners. It's got to stop.

JAMIE:

Agreed and agreed.

KITTY:

All clear in there?

PAT:

Right.—Who's coming this afternoon?

KITTY:

Just Peter Baillie, you said—and the Irish Minister at ten in the morning.

She goes out into the Library.

PAT:

Good.

JAMIE *gives him his whisky-and-soda.*

That's a good dress.

JAMIE:

I think so, too.

PAT:

And a good girl in it. Nut brown maid, thou hast a slender slender waist. How are you liking your life these days, Jamieson?

JAMIE:

Enchanted with it. The formula's perfect, Pat.

PAT:

Make with the Head instead of the Heart: who shall say us nay?

89

JAMIE:

Not me: I know my luck. You haven't just made this house over, you know—you've made me over with it.

PAT:

You?—You're your own special creation and will remain so, praise God. I'd say we were putting on quite a good show, though.

JAMIE *laughs*.

JAMIE:

—Except that Martha tells me that she and Quent have decided to stick just on account of the pretty picture *we* make.

PAT:

It's nice to know we're that good an example.

JAMIE:

After a moment.

Father always said that people learned much better by example than by—by precept.

PAT:

Did he?

JAMIE:

Yes. Do you believe that?

PAT:

Why, I suppose in certain—

JAMIE:

In a rush.

Because I hope you do! Because I—well, I know the terrible time you're having convincing Baillie that—

90

you know—that the English and Irish just can't get together alone by themselves—you know—without help from us, and—and when I heard he was coming this afternoon I got a crazy idea that maybe if —well, yesterday I located an Irishman—an awfully nice one that I used to know in Dublin—Harry and I stayed with him once during Horse Show Week— well, he's here. So I telephoned his hotel and left word asking him to come in today and—

> *She swallows.*

—and also nice Richard Hood of the British to—to well, you know—just to meet and talk for Baillie's benefit.

PAT:

Why, you scheming little—

JAMIE:

I'm sorry. You were out somewhere and I didn't know how to reach you.

> PAT *reflects.*

PAT:

Of course they'll probably get on together like angels.

JAMIE:

Oh, wouldn't that be awful!

PAT:

But maybe not, maybe not.

JAMIE:

What worries me is, Baillie's such a sphinx, how will we know if it brings him around?

PAT:

Easy: he'd probably start calling me by my first name and ask me to save him the waltz.

He sighs wearily.

JAMIE:

You *are* tired, Pat. You need a holiday.

PAT:

When do we get that wedding-trip we missed?

JAMIE:

When do you get a spare moment for one?

PAT:

Hot Springs, where are you? Lord, how things pile up in this town. Have we got a free evening to-night, by any chance?

JAMIE:

So far as I know. I meant to check with Kitty.

PAT:

I hope she's working out as well for you as she is for me.

JAMIE:

I don't know how we managed without her.

PAT:

You'd never suspect she had a life of her own, would you?

JAMIE *widens her eyes unconvincingly.*

JAMIE:

Oh no—oh, dear no!

PAT:

Ah-ha!

92

JAMIE:

Oh-ho!

PAT *indicates the white violets.*

PAT:

—I see you've been bunched again.

JAMIE:

He keeps sending them. I don't know why.

PAT:

But you like them, don't you?

JAMIE:

Why, yes—the fact is, I do.

PAT:

Maybe you miss love more than you think, Jamie.

JAMIE:

Pat—what are you talking about!

PAT:

But don't confuse it with love-making, will you?

JAMIE:

You keep forgetting the woman of the world you've made me over into.

PAT:

I'll miss her on this tour that's ahead of me.

JAMIE:

Two whole months. Do you really feel you have to do it?

PAT:

I know them in Ireland but I don't know them here. We've got twenty million of 'em—all fighters and all with a just grudge. I want to know what they're thinking at first hand.

JAMIE:

After a moment.

Are you sure that's the only reason you're getting out?

PAT:

"Getting out"? That's a strange way to put it. What do you mean?

JAMIE *smiles faintly.*

JAMIE:

I know about the lovely refugee that arrived last week, Pat.

PAT:

The—?

JAMIE:

Your Lila—Lila Vine—Lila Hattersfield now, isn't it? With her child—and divorced—and staying with the Rumsons. I know she wants to see you, because she telephoned twice when you were out. And I—

PAT:

Well, what about it?

JAMIE:

—And I thought the trip might have something to do with it—no—don't stop me!—with not wanting to meet up with her. And—and I just wanted you to know that it's all right with me if you do. I wouldn't mind. I wouldn't worry. Why should I?—And I

94

particularly wouldn't like to think that you'd run away just on account of—

PAT *rises.*

PAT:

Run away? What are you talking about?

JAMIE:

I only thought—

PAT:

Well, you needn't! When you catch me running away from someone—. Listen, Jamie: just get it through your head once and for all—

JAMIE:

—And just you be sure of your motives, Pat. And be sure for yourself that my head's all I've got to get it through—and that it's through that already.

PAT:

Then why, for the love of—

He stops and turns away.

JAMIE:

The love of what, Pat? What love have *we* two anything to do with?

PETER BAILLIE *comes in from the Hall.*

Oh, thank Heaven—at last an American!

PETER:

You nice girl, you. How are you, I needn't ask?

She goes to make a drink for him.

JAMIE:

We've missed you, Mr. Baillie.

PETER:

I've missed myself. Well, Jamieson—how's it been going with you? And how's it with your famous time-sense?

PAT:

Fine, thanks. Both still functioning.

PETER:

Sometimes I think Time is fooling us, these days: that the world has taken to spinning around the sun at quite a dizzy new speed.

JAMIE:

Oh, don't say that! That's terrible.

PETER:

I see little on the horizon that is not. And the waste that goes on here—the absolute, wanton waste!

He lights a cigarette.

Well—I suppose it's something to go down in history as the country with the swellest swill on earth.

PAT:

What does the President think of the outlook?

PETER:

He's thinking.

PAT:

In the second-last letter I wrote you, I said—

PETER:

He read it. He's reading them now, you'll be glad to know.

PAT:

Then why doesn't he do something about it?

PETER:

If it's your proposed swing around the country to sound out the Harps that's on your mind—

PAT:

That's one of the things that's there.

PETER:

—A quiet official sanction is still possible.

JAMIE:

You mean it?

PETER:

It being understood, of course, that if there was one spot of personal publicity, he'd be disavowed at once.

PAT:

There wouldn't be a spot.

>JAMIE, *returning with the drink, stops suddenly.*

JAMIE:

Oh dear—

PAT:

What's wrong?

JAMIE:

Nothing—not a thing.

>*She gives* PETER *the drink.*

Pat—is Paul Carrel's number Dupont or Decatur?

PAT:

Dupont. Why?

JAMIE:

I—I want to call him about something. Excuse me?
She moves toward the Library.

PAT:

Two-one-seven-one.

JAMIE:

—Dupont. Hello, Paul. This is Jamie again.
She goes out. PETER *settles himself with his
drink and gazes at* PAT.

PETER:

Well—what are the big new empirical ideas today?

PAT:

Empirical? None that I've ever had. Empire's the
real sin at the bottom of this—Germany's for going
after it, Britain's for holding onto it.

PETER:

—Except that Ulster doesn't want her independence.

PAT:

Nor did the Tories here, back in the first place.

PETER:

Hardly the same, would you say?

PAT:

Yes, I'd say. Very much the.

PETER:

There'd be trouble, you know.

PAT:

We also had a touch of that between the North and
the South once.

PETER:

Just what would you like us to ask the British to do?

PAT:

I wouldn't like us to ask them anything. I'd like us to tell them for once.

PETER:

What?

PAT:

First of all, to drop their damned condescension—and deal with the Irish as they would with any strong independent nation—which they are.

PETER:

Strong?

PAT:

In their hearts—where it counts! Lord—I know we're *all* wrong now, the three of us. But if, with the same language, we can't get to understand each other and arrive somewhere, what the hell hope is there for afterwards? How many times do you want this in a generation?

PETER:

Those two don't need us butting in. They can work it out between themselves.

PAT:

They haven't been able to in some seven hundred years.

PETER:

They will now. I'm convinced of it. So is Himself.

PAT:

The trouble with you both is, you don't understand the difference a difference in temperaments makes.

PETER:

Dear old Human Relations again.

PAT:

That's it!

PETER:

I wish I knew how really wise you are—or how much you're just another bright boy who wants to mix up in things.

PAT:

And I wish I knew whether you and the rest of the Big Shots I've been dealing with here are the simple-minded, slow, every-day sons of—human beings you seem to be—or whether all governments are like that when you know them!

JAMIE *reenters from the Library.*

JAMIE:

He's gone out. Oh dear—

BAILLIE:

Simultaneously.

I've told you we've planted control of this in the Navy Department.

PAT:

Then why can't I get through to them? Why won't Grant Vincent see me?

PETER:

I asked him. He said he hasn't any use for Euro-peanized Americans.

PAT:

So that's what I am.

PETER:

No—but Vincent has great prejudices. That's part of his value.

JAMIE:

Grant Vincent? I used to know him. He used to hunt with Harry and me.

PAT:

Fine!—And now I hunt him.

JAMIE:

I wonder if—

>   ANNA *comes into the Hall doorway.*

—Yes, Anna?

ANNA:

Sir Richard Hood.

>   HOOD *enters. He is forty or forty-five, like-*
>   *able, ruddy, ebullient.*

HOOD:

Hello, Pat. I'm late. Awful rush to get to dinner. Make me a Scotch and soda, will you? No ice.

>   *To* JAMIE.

Hello, you lovely creature. Why don't you leave this coarse American and come and live with me on my ancestral estate, just sold for taxes?

JAMIE:

Am I invited?

HOOD:

Every time. Bless my soul, it's pleasant here—calm and tranquil and serene. And cool, too.—Just saw a friend of yours, Pat—asked after you—Mrs. Hattersfield—wants to see you.

PAT:

Well, I don't want to see her.

HOOD:

Silly. Contrary. Foolish. She's charming. Why not, old boy?

PAT:

I just don't.

HOOD:

But to my mind that's madness. That's what causes wars. That's the kind of thing that—

He sees PETER.

Who's this?

JAMIE:

Haven't you met Mr. Baillie? I thought of course—

HOOD:

Mr. Peter Baillie? No—I can't say I have. Is this him? How do you do? So you're actually Peter Baillie—

PETER:

My parents thought so.

HOOD:

—Should have known you from your photographs

—the fatigued, intent look. The brain that never sleeps. The ascetic expression. The—er—the—

PETER:

Hood, to hear you maunder on, anyone would think you were a complete nitwit. Fortunately, I know different.

> *Again* ANNA *appears, a visiting-card in hand.*

ANNA:

Mr. Robert Emmet Riordan.

> *She goes out as* EMMET *comes in. He is a middle-aged Irishman, distinguished in looks and merry of eye. His accent is very slight.*

EMMET:

God bless you all.

JAMIE:

Emmet! I'm *so* glad—

EMMET:

The pleasure is my own, intact and undivided.

> *He goes to her.*

Jamie Rowan!—And I'll steal a small kiss, if you don't mind.

JAMIE:

I'd mind if you didn't.

> *He kisses her on both cheeks. She explains:*

—But it's Jamie Jamieson, now.

EMMET:

To be sure, to be sure!

He turns and looks at HOOD *and* PAT.

Which of them would it be?

JAMIE:

Two guesses.—That's Mr. Peter Baillie, resting.

EMMET *moves toward* PAT *and* HOOD, *nodding to* PETER *as he passes him.*

EMMET:

Mr. Baillie—an event!

PETER:

Headlines, Mr. Riordan.

EMMET *puts on his spectacles, glances briefly at* HOOD, *then peers at* PAT *through them.*

EMMET:

I believe I knew your father. Did I?

PAT:

I wouldn't be surprised.

EMMET *grasps his hand warmly.*

EMMET:

You favor him. Up Jamieson!

PAT:

Up Riordan!

JAMIE:

And how's your sweet wife, Emmet—and all the children—and the dogs and the horses and that lovely old place?

EMMET:

Unanimous! Not a stone nor a feature changed, praise be to Glory.

PAT:

Mr. Riordan—Sir Richard Hood.

> *The* TWO MEN *bow.* PAT *explains to* EM-
> MET:

—Sir Richard's Economic Warfare.

EMMET:

Oh, are they fighting with economics now?

> HOOD *laughs.*

HOOD:

I love the Irish. My great grandmother was kissed by an Irish Earl once—and here I am!

EMMET:

My own great grandfather was kicked by an English horse—but it left no impression at all.

PAT:

What'll you have? Martini? Whisky and soda? I have Irish—what about a spot of my namesake?

EMMET:

That would be heaven.

> PAT *goes to make it for him.* EMMET *and*
> HOOD *are gazing at each other,* PETER
> *watching them closely.*

Are you here for long, Sir Richard?

HOOD:

Duration, I expect. Of course I nip back and forth a bit.—And you?

EMMET:

A man cannot be sure.

HOOD:

Pleasant country on the whole, don't you think?

EMMET:

A clean, well-lighted place.

HOOD:

You're from the so-called Irish Free State, I take it?

EMMET:

You take it correctly—from Dublin, so-called.

PAT *returns with his drink.*

PAT:

I made it half and half—chiefly half.

EMMET:

My heart's thanks.

HOOD:

Dublin—ah, yes.—Was there once—charming little city.

EMMET:

My favorite among the metropoli of the world.

HOOD:

How'd you like it if Jerry had a go at it?

EMMET:

My dismay would be keen.

HOOD:

What's to stop him?

EMMET:

Me and me fellow residents, I expect.

HOOD:

But with what?

EMMET:

We still have some small arms and general apparatus and useful paraphernalia left over since the Trouble. Of course, we could use more.

HOOD:

I know, old man—but you're not willing to pay.

EMMET:

We're willing. We have the money.

HOOD:

Money's no good these days.

EMMET:

Good God, man, you shock me! Then what is?

HOOD:

Those naval bases of yours, y' know: we could use 'em.

PETER:

You bet your hat you could.

EMMET:

We're a neutral nation, and firmly united in our neutrality.

PETER:

United? What about Ulster?

HOOD:

Ulster's ours!

EMMET:

—I am speaking of Eire. The six counties and that

black act of malfeasance, the Partition, is another subject entirely, and a bitter one.

HOOD:

All the same, as Jamieson here is so fond of reminding us, you're our left flank. And if Jerry's mad enough to attempt to invade again, it's you who are likely to get it first.

EMMET:

Is it, now?

HOOD:

I'd like to make you see sense about this thing.

EMMET:

I'm all ears, Sir Richard.

> ANNA *appears in the Hall doorway.*

ANNA:

Excuse me, Madam. It's Mr. Carrel to see you.
> *And goes out again.*

JAMIE:

Please stay here. I'll take him into the little room.

PAT:

No—we'll move our argument out to the terrace. Come on, boys.—Mr. Baillie?

PETER:

Wouldn't miss it.

HOOD:

Argument, my eye—but how'd you like to be a German Gibraltar?

108

EMMET:

Argument, your granny—but neither would we care to be an international cockpit.

> *They go out ahead of* PAT, *who turns as* CARREL *comes in from the Hall.*

PAT:

Hello, Paul. Have a drink. Everything's there—except Vichy.

> *He follows* PETER, EMMET *and* HOOD *to the terrace, leaving* JAMIE *with* CARREL.

JAMIE:

What did you decide, Paul? Tell me quickly.

CARREL:

I shall tell you in my own time. I'm furious with you.

JAMIE:

Really? For what?

CARREL:

For making me into—what was it that columnist called me?—into an Indian Giver.

JAMIE:

Then you did take back the story about Pat!

CARREL:

For the first time in my journalistic life, I have turned softie.

JAMIE:

No! You've turned true friend! It would have been just pure poison at this point.

CARREL:

—Coming at me over a cup of tea—with a dry, analytical American mind. You should be ashamed. How was it possible?

JAMIE:

Sometime you must visit the State of Maine, Paul.

CARREL:

—But your estimate of Pat—your cool, detached survey of his virtues *and* his faults—it was quite surprising from a wife, quite amazing.

JAMIE:

Calm and dispassionate.

CARREL:

Exactly. Also most unusual, from a wife of a husband. That is, unless—

He stops himself and begins to watch her more closely.

JAMIE:

Unless what?

CARREL:

Never in my life will I understand American marriages.

JAMIE:

They're really very simple. At least ours is.

CARREL:

They are so selfish, while they last. They remove such attractive people from circulation.

JAMIE:

Ours isn't selfish. We've always been blissfully independent.

CARREL:

Will you lunch with me Saturday?

JAMIE:

Saturday? Let's see—Pat has to be in New York then and—well, Saturday I'd planned to spend the day at my farm. Why don't we drive out—and you lunch with me there?

CARREL:

Alone?

JAMIE:

Except for the horses and pigs and things—why not?

Suddenly she laughs.

CARREL:

What are you laughing at?

JAMIE:

You and your primness. Do you mind?

CARREL:

Primness, is it?

JAMIE.

Primness it is!

CARREL:

I'm glad you can laugh, Jamie.

JAMIE:

I do lots. Why shouldn't I?

CARREL:

Because all at once I see why you were able to do with me what you did for Pat. He could not have done it for himself—no, nor you for him—unless for this curious fact.

JAMIE:

Curious fact? That sounds awfully mysterious.

CARREL:

Believe me, it is—or was.

JAMIE:

I suppose I'm just being stupid, but—

> *From the terrace is heard the sound of a slap followed by a surprised grunt.*

CARREL:

What is it?

JAMIE:

I can't imagine. I—

> EMMET *comes in from the terrace, adjusting his cuffs.*

Emmet, what in the world happened?

EMMET:

He grew a trifle *too* condescending, my dear.

> HOOD *comes in after him, with* PAT *and* PETER *following.*

HOOD:

The scoundrel! The ignorant, low-life, rascally bog-trotter!

PETER:

Well, of all the—

JAMIE:

—But Mr. Baillie!

PETER:

Why two grown-up, civilized human beings can't
arrive at something constructive—

PAT:

But they just don't seem able to, do they?—Not
without help.

HOOD:

When you ask me to your house again, sir—

PAT:

Oh, come on, Richard—or I'll sock you myself!

EMMET:

The house is too small for the two of us, so good
evening to you—and God bless you all.

He goes out, into the Hall.

PETER:

Come along, Hood—I'll drop you. I want to talk
manners to both of you.

They start out.

HOOD:

If you knew what we've put up with from them,
ever since Cromwell was a pup—

He goes out. PETER *turns in the Hallway.*

PETER:

Oh—er—Pat—

PAT:

Yes, Peter?

PETER:

There's a little free time at four tomorrow. Care to drop around?

PAT:

Thanks. I'd be glad to.

> PETER *goes out.* PAT *turns to* JAMIE.

Nice work, you politician's daughter!

> *And follows* PETER. JAMIE *smiles at* CARREL.

JAMIE:

Another story for you, Paul—but you're not going to use it.

CARREL:

But my dear—!

> *He looks at her, and then adds:*

No, Jamie.

JAMIE:

Thanks again. Pat also thanks you.

CARREL:

Very odd, how it is that you do not pale out before that very vital and vigorous young man—odd, how he brings you into perspective.

JAMIE:

Is that the "curious fact"?

CARREL:

No—the curious fact is the very curious one of a lovely girl who does not love her husband.

JAMIE:

Who doesn't—? What are you talking about?

CARREL:

—And who doubtless never has. Nor he you, possibly. Amid all this plenty—starvation.—Not curious?

JAMIE:

Honestly, I never heard such downright—

CARREL:

I was stupid not to know at once—because otherwise it would not have been possible for you to speak of him as you did this afternoon. Angrily, yes—maliciously, yes—tear him to pieces—call him all the names in the world—yes, still possible—but not possible so—so what-you-say—"calm and dispassionate."

JAMIE:

After a moment.

All right—that's what persuaded you, isn't it? Suppose we happen to believe that in times like these two people can help each other much more if they *aren't* in love?

CARREL:

Very perverse, very interesting.—But two Americans?

JAMIE:

What's that got to do with it?

CARREL:

Such idealists—so sentimental.

JAMIE:

That's a lot of talk. You won't find harder heads anywhere.—And as for your so-called "starvation," if Pat and I aren't a hundred times happier than any number who married for— I tell you it works!

> CARREL *laughs.*

CARREL:

Sweet Jamie!

JAMIE:

So if it does, what's the difference?

CARREL:

None—except to me.—Until Saturday, then?

JAMIE:

Saturday? Why the fact is, I'm afraid, after all, I—

CARREL:

My primness, did you say?

> *She looks at him.*

JAMIE:

How foolish I am.

> *She holds out her hand to him.*

—Until Saturday, Paul.

> *He takes her face in his hands and kisses her.*

CARREL:

Oh, my sweet.

> *He releases her and goes out. For a moment* JAMIE *stands appalled, then smiles, tosses the violets in the air and catches them.* PAT *reenters and goes swiftly to her.*

PAT:

What an Irishman! What an Englishman! And *what* a girl! Oh, bless your heart, Jamie.

He kisses her, then stands off and looks at her, puzzled.

What's up, dear? What's wrong?

JAMIE:

Nothing—not a thing. It just seems that it's my afternoon for being kissed.

Curtain

ACT II

SCENE 2

> *It is two months later, about half-past eleven on a night in late June, the same year. Only two small lamps are lighted in the Living-room, which is the same as in the preceding scene. One of the doors to the terrace is open a little way, giving a glimpse of the bright moonlit night outside. Through this door an occasional puff of breeze blows the window-curtain against one of the lamps.*
>
> *After a moment* PAT *and* KITTY *appear in the Hall doorway.* KITTY *is in street clothes and a hat.* PAT'S *hat also is still upon his head and he carries a briefcase. He glances about him at the room.*

PAT:

—A long time, but much the same. Still a handsome room in any light.

KITTY:

Shall I switch on some more?

PAT:

No—leave it as it is, dim and religious.

> *He comes down into the room,* KITTY *following.*

KITTY:

I'm not a nosey girl as a rule—but what's it all about?

PAT:

It? What—

He tosses his hat down upon the piano.

KITTY:

Your coming back from your trip a whole week ahead of time—your wire to me to meet you, without a word to anyone. I figured that the "anyone" included Jamie. Right?

PAT:

Right as rain. I did an eight weeks' job in seven and thought I'd surprise her. Where is she?

KITTY:

I don't know. In bed, don't you suppose? It's past eleven.

PAT:

Where's Anna? Where the hell *is* everyone?

KITTY:

You didn't ring, you know. You let yourself in.

PAT:

And for what?

He presses the button beside the fireplace.

KITTY:

What was your trip like, Pat? What did you gather from your Irish-American brothers?

PAT:

Well, I'll tell you: the ones in Boston are stubborner than the ones in Brooklyn—and the ones in Chicago are less stubborn, but more arrogant—and the ones in San Francisco are the most stubbornly arrogant bastards I've ever come up against.

KITTY:

It doesn't sound hopeful.

PAT:

Not for bringing pressure on the homeland, no— pretty discouraging. But they're mine and I'm theirs and I love 'em! What news around here—any?

KITTY:

Nothing that I haven't wired or written you. Peter Baillie phoned again a couple of times this week.

PAT:

What about?

KITTY:

He wouldn't admit it, but I think that he and Prexy miss your letters.

PAT:

He'll get one in the morning that will stand his hair on end. Can you type it up tonight and deliver it by hand?

KITTY:

The usual length?

PAT:

A little longer.

KITTY:

What must be, must be.

PAT:

I've signed three blank sheets: middle, towards bottom, and bottom.

KITTY:

You're learning.

PAT:

Still no word from Grant Vincent, I suppose.

KITTY:

No—for him, you don't exist.

PAT:

I've got to get to him. I must. It's essential. This is still a Navy job—though it could change. Oh, boy —just couldn't it!

> ANNA *comes into the Hall doorway. She is clutching a gray wrapper around her.*

Hello, Anna.

ANNA:

Good evening, sir. We weren't expecting you till—

PAT:

I'm sorry to have disturbed you—but is Mrs. Jamieson in?

ANNA:

No, sir—that is, I don't think so, not yet. She called from the country just after dinner and asked me to pack her a bag for a day in New York.

PAT:

Off tonight, is she?

ANNA:

A late train, she said. And—well, it's still beside the door where I left it—her bag, I mean.

PAT:

So I'll catch her in time. Good. Has she been long at the farm?

ANNA:

Oh no—she just went out for the day today—she and Mr. Carrel and I think some others.

She goes out.

PAT:

"And she thinks some others."

KITTY:

What's wrong with a little jaunt to the country? It's not the first time.

PAT:

True—our French friend has been quite a good little chauffeur this spring.

KITTY:

It's all over now. He's going back to La Belle by Clipper tomorrow.

PAT:

Yes: so Richard Hood phoned me this afternoon.

KITTY:

And is that maybe also why you came back ahead of time?

He turns and looks at her. She meets his gaze steadily. He smiles.

PAT:

You're a bright one, Miss Trim.

KITTY:

And so is Carrel—at his true life-work, l'amour. I'm glad you don't underrate him.

> *He moves away from her toward the sofa.*

PAT:

I know Paul of yore: descended from a long and unbroken line of heels, he dwells contentedly in his ivory sewer.

> *From the sofa, he picks up a silk scarf which has been thrown there with a small, faded bunch of white violets. He shakes the scarf open and examines it.*

What a nice scarf of Jamie's. She wears them tied around her bonny locks when motoring—*très chic, comme une paysanne.* This must be a new one—scenes of La Belle: Deauville—Cannes—Trouville—*toutes les Villes Elegantes.* And rather a limp little bunch of white violets. Behold the drama of the inanimate object.

> *He drops the violets upon the scarf and turns to her again.*

What are you thinking, Kitty?

KITTY:

Thoughts. But I'm sure she's been all right—at least so far.

PAT:

You'd better run along. It's late.

KITTY:

If I'm to get the letter out, I had.

She moves toward the open terrace-door.

Delivered by hand, you said?

PAT:

I hate to ask it, but it's important.

KITTY:

I hate to do it, but consider it done.

She moves the blowing curtain away from the lamp and smooths it down.

Sooner or later this lamp's going to give up the fight. You've got enough air, haven't you?

PAT:

Plenty.

She opens the door a trifle wider and looks out along the terrace, exclaiming softly:

KITTY:

What a really heavenly night! There's not a single—

Suddenly she stops, waits a moment, still looking out. Then she closes the door very carefully.

—damn cloud in the sky. I hope it's not this way over Moscow, poor thing.

She comes up to PAT with extreme casualness.

Well—goodnight, Boss. Why don't you go up and get out of your traveling clothes and into a bath and a wrapper? I'll leave a note for Jamie in the hall, if you like.

He looks at her quizzically.

PAT:

Would you really do that?

KITTY:

Sure. What do you want me to say?

PAT:

Really and truly would you?

KITTY:

Look: what *is* this?

PAT:

Cross your heart and hope to die?

KITTY:

Constant association with your friends, the Harps, seems to have made you a little whimsical, Master.

PAT:

What was it you saw?

KITTY:

Saw? Where?

PAT:

On the terrace.

KITTY:

On the—? Why, nothing. What would I have?

PAT:

Not a little love-scene, possibly? Not a serious one, of course—

KITTY:

Honestly, I haven't the remotest idea what you're—. Now, listen, you—

PAT:

—Just a simple, tender one. The arms around—the head upon the shoulder—the temperate kiss.

KITTY:

How can you be so cold about it?

PAT:

Or was it so temperate? Was it perhaps the prelude to an even darker deed?

Suddenly she grasps his arm.

KITTY:

Do something, Pat. Do it quickly. She's really been desperately lonely and he—Carrel, I mean—the fallen country, the flight back to ruins—the never, never meet again—it's all too romantic—bag packed at the door—it's too damned dangerous. And you know why? She's different from me. She couldn't ever be —you know—casual about it. You know, don't you? She'd never be the same again.

PAT:

No—she'd never be the same again. Not Jamie.

KITTY:

Pat—

PAT:

—And she's rather nice as she is, isn't she?

KITTY:

Yes—yes—she's the nicest girl I know.—Pat, don't rave, don't rant—don't blaze with jealousy—above all, don't humiliate her. You won't, will you, Pat?

PAT:

No—none of that. I wouldn't know how to. Look, Kitty—it's about time you got straight on something: Jamie and I have an odd sort of relationship. It doesn't allow for jealousy, but it does allow for helping each other out of jams. I think that's what this is. I just don't think the guy's good enough.—So I proceed to act. Does that seem cold to you, too?

KITTY:

I simply don't understand a word you've been saying—

> PAT *waits an instant, then gestures.*

PAT:

Let it go. Maybe it's just as well.

KITTY:

But *I'd* like to say one fairly brutal thing if I may.

PAT:

Go ahead.

KITTY:

I think maybe with all your work and your trips away and your general preoccupation you haven't been much of a husband here lately. I think maybe Jamie's is a case of substituting something for something that's missing.

PAT:

Do you, Kitty?

KITTY:

You know, while men seem to be reasonably intelligent about their own so-called love-life, they're apt at times to be awfully stupid about a girl's.

PAT:

Thanks for the tip.

KITTY:

And there are very few of us in this world who, under certain circumstances, aren't vulnerable to someone. Believe me, I know that.

PAT:

So, it would seem, do certain Frenchmen.

KITTY:

So goodnight, Pat. Shall I come in the morning?

PAT:

At the same time, if you will.

KITTY:

Goodnight, then.

PAT:

Goodnight, Kitty. God love you.

> *She is gone.* PAT *ponders a moment, then puts on his hat again, turns on the lamp, seats himself at the piano and starts playing.* JAMIE *and* CARREL *come in suddenly from the terrace.*

JAMIE:

Pat!

PAT:

Hello, little fellow.

JAMIE:

But why didn't you let me know you were coming?

128

PAT:

I thought I'd surprise you.—Lord, how I've missed this blessed piano—and you too, Jamie.

> *He tosses his hat down upon the piano again, rises from it and kisses her briefly.*

How are you, Paul?

CARREL:

Splendidly, thanks. We're just back from a fine long day in the country.

PAT:

Nothing like it. You both look fine, all right.

> *He goes to make himself a drink.*

JAMIE:

You seem a little worn, yourself. Was it a hard trip?

PAT:

Yes—but interesting. I learned quite a lot.—This is my first real one since I left.

> *He raises his glass.*

I found that when studying the Irish, it's best to stick to beer. Otherwise they study you in your relation to the floor. What's new around—anything?

JAMIE:

Well, for one thing, it seems that Paul is off on the Clipper tomorrow.

PAT:

Now where did I hear that?

CARREL:

I don't see how you could have. I didn't know it myself until last evening.

PAT:

Word travels fast, doesn't it?—I'm glad it's not for long, though.

CARREL:

Well—that is to say—

JAMIE:

But isn't it? I—I thought it was for good.

PAT:

Funny, I understood it was just to check with his home-office and then to come straight back.

CARREL:

Not at all.

PAT:

But aren't you booked to return at the same pretty clip the first of August?

CARREL:

That is just a formality, just—you know—just in case.

PAT:

Well anyhow, let's hope you make it. We'll miss you around here, Paul. What in the world will the girls do without you?

CARREL:

What girls are those?

PAT:

Oh, the tall ones, the short ones, the dark ones, the

fair ones—the whole garland of girls from eighteen to forty.

CARREL:

Are you by any chance trying to be disagreeable?

JAMIE:

Yes, Pat—your manner's odd, to say the least. What is it? Why not out with it, if—if there's something, you—

PAT:

Me? Disagreeable? On Paul's last night in Washington for maybe a month?—On the contrary!

> *To* CARREL.

How about opening a bottle of wine?

CARREL:

Not for me, thanks.

PAT:

Darling, why don't you run up to New York tomorrow and see him off?

JAMIE:

Why—I really hadn't thought of it.

PAT:

I can't make it myself—and I *would* like to have the family represented.

CARREL:

Come, if you would. You know I'd like so much to have you.

JAMIE:

I'm afraid I'd only be in the way.

PAT:

Don't you believe it! Would she, Paul?

CARREL:

I can think of nothing that would make my leave-taking pleasanter.—Now I'm afraid I must go.

PAT:

Go? Don't think of it, you old night-owl. I'm off myself in about ten minutes.

To JAMIE.

Is my car in the garage, I hope?

JAMIE:

Why yes, I think so.—But off where? Where to? You've only just got here.

PAT:

I know. It's a bore. I meant to tell you: Hugh Nelson's at Hot Springs from Geneva, and I've got to see him. So I thought if I ran down tonight—it's only about four hours, on a good night, with good going—

JAMIE:

Four hours! It's over two hundred—!

PAT:

It's such a fine, bright one—did you ever see such a moon? Care to come along?—But of course not, you're busy.—Those were great days in Geneva, back in '36, weren't they, Paul?

CARREL:

I had almost forgotten them,

132

PAT:

Not me!

> *To* JAMIE.

We used to walk the Esplanade before the Court of
The League for hours—and sit in cafés for hours
more—and talk philosophy—chiefly the philosophy
of love, eh, Paul?

CARREL:

I was a very young man, then.

PAT:

You were thirty-eight, if you were a day.

> *To* JAMIE.

He claimed it was his own philosophy, though I
suspect it derived from Montaigne and a few
others.

JAMIE:

What was it?

PAT:

Do you think she's old enough, Paul? Women are
pretty humorless about such things, you know.
They seem to lack that saving grace.

JAMIE:

Not all of us.

PAT:

It was very simple: "Of a divine simplicity," Paul
used to say. It was that love—I must get this straight
—it was that love, so-called, was a mere appetite like
any other. And that a man, so-called, could not be
expected to subsist on cakes and ale, *or* beef and

burgundy. Variety in diet was the great desideratum, whatever the care and patience required in preparing the—dish. What was your phrase, Paul? Oh, yes—"*La plus difficile, est la—*" hell, we're Americans!—"The more difficult she is, the more delicious."

JAMIE:

>*After a moment.*

I see. That is, I think I do. And now shall I laugh?

PAT:

Everything has its funny side—though the humor be grim, at times.

>*He takes his briefcase from the table.*

I've got to dig up some odd scraps of paper and be on my way.

>*And moves toward the Library.*

There'll be nothing I need, Jamie. My bag's O.K.— Bon voyage, Paul. Give us a ring the moment you're back.—

>*He goes out. Slowly* JAMIE *turns to* CARREL.

CARREL:

My point of view is my point of view, and will remain so.

JAMIE:

I respect it for what it is. I even understand it now.

CARREL:

When he has left—shall I come back for you—or will you come to me?

JAMIE:

Not either. Because it seems I'm not going to New York with you after all, Paul.

CARREL:

And why? Because he—because you—?

JAMIE:

—Because of many things. Because I—because suddenly all our—tendernesses of these last days—because all at once I know they were no more to me than—bits of bread and sips of wine to someone who's been starving.

CARREL:

You turn his little speech very conveniently to your own uses.

JAMIE:

I think he meant it for me. You see, it's the difference between a marriage—and what you and I might have.

CARREL:

Did I ever pretend we'd have anything else?

JAMIE:

No—and now, somehow, I'm thankful for that.

CARREL:

But if he knows and gives us carte blanche—a clear field, as he has, I fail to see why we should not—

JAMIE:

But you failed to see something else—or to hear it.

CARREL:

And what?

JAMIE:

That when he drives alone at night, he drives very fast—and that he's my husband, and I don't care to risk him—and that he asked me to go with him.

CARREL:

There was another invitation, accepted before.

JAMIE:

—And I'm not even begging your pardon.

CARREL:

—Sweet Jamie. I'll tell you a secret: one day both of you may be grateful to me. Funny?

JAMIE:

To you? Grateful?

CARREL:

Ah, my dear—grant me my small consolation.

> *He kisses her tenderly.*

There—no goodbyes. And don't think I have ever thought of you lightly. Remember me, Jamie—I shall remember you.

> *He goes out, murmuring:*

Funny—so funny—

> JAMIE *leans against the table, her head bent, her shoulders shaking.*

JAMIE:

Funny—funny—

> PAT *reenters from the Library. He sees her, hesitates a moment, then drops his briefcase on the table and goes to her.*

PAT:

Don't take it so hard, Jamie. He'll be back.

JAMIE:

I'm not taking it any way. I'm just laughing.

PAT:

Why?

JAMIE:

Maybe because I *do* have that saving grace.

PAT:

Good stuff.

> *He looks at his watch.*

Well, if I go, I'll be back by tomorrow, anyway.

JAMIE:

It's tomorrow already. Oh, Pat, I—

PAT:

Let it go, Jamie.

JAMIE:

But, Pat, I'm in a—I think I'm in an awfully strange
state.

PAT:

—Of suspension. I know. I've been there. It's loneliness does it. Two months is two months.

JAMIE:

I just don't understand myself. Paul—he—I—

PAT:

He's a pretty fascinating fellow, isn't he? I don't
wonder they fall, do you?

JAMIE:

I've got to tell you something—

PAT:

I'm not sure I want to hear it. In fact, I'm certain I don't.

JAMIE:

That doesn't matter.

PAT:

What! Have I no authority in your own house?

JAMIE:

I nearly did, Pat.

PAT:

What?

JAMIE:

Fall.

PAT:

For Paul?

> *He laughs shortly and moves to the piano.*

Ridiculous!

JAMIE:

I know. But it's true.

PAT:

Well, if it is, in the first place I don't believe it, in the second, I don't want to hear about it—and in the third, a miss is as good as a mile.

> *He begins to play the piano softly, improvising vaguely descriptive music of the scene as it follows.*

JAMIE:

You don't think I'm serious—

138

PAT:

Not a bit. You're not the falling type. You're like
the Tower of Pisa: you may have certain leanings,
but you always remain upright.

JAMIE:

I saw it once.

PAT:

And a mighty impressive sight, too!

JAMIE:

I didn't think so. I didn't like it.—And I don't think
I like you thinking of me as it.

PAT:

I think other things, too.

JAMIE:

All so noble?

PAT:

Mostly.

JAMIE:

I'm coming with you, Pat.

PAT:

Where to?

JAMIE:

Hot Springs. Hot Springs eternal—

PAT:

But I'm not going.

JAMIE:

Since when?

PAT:

Since I just thought it over.

JAMIE:

—But I wanted to go with you!

PAT:

Sorry. I've got to be here in the morning. The President's going to need to see me—the week-end on "The Potomac" probably. Once he reads this last letter to Peter—

> JAMIE *comes up to him, stands over him, speaks down to him in a voice curiously charged, curiously intense for what she is saying:*

JAMIE:

But I desperately wanted to! For days, for weeks, I've looked forward to it. It's filled all my thoughts: I've gone to bed at night hoping for it. I've waked in the night, thinking we were there—and again in the morning, still dreaming of it. It's—it's so nearby, Pat.

PAT:

No time at all, on a good night.

JAMIE:

Less than that—on any night.

PAT:

Mighty pretty country around there—

JAMIE:

I think it must be heavenly.

> *He plays a run on the piano.*

PAT:

Here we are, just rounding the bend. Made it in nothing flat.

JAMIE:

Oh, I'm so glad—I did want so to be here!

PAT:

Do you feel the altitude?

JAMIE:

I thought it was my heart.

PAT:

The Homestead: a very respectable place, on the whole.

JAMIE:

I—I hope they have room for us.

PAT:

I don't know: this is still their spring season.
She comes round the piano and faces him.

JAMIE:

Is there someone at the desk?

PAT:

Right here.

JAMIE:

Good evening, whatever your name is.

PAT:

Good evenin', Miss.

JAMIE:

"Missus," if you don't mind.

PAT:

Not in the least. On the continent.

JAMIE:

Pleasant evening.

PAT:

Very.

JAMIE:

A charming place you have here—

PAT:

—Seldom a complaint.

JAMIE:

Have you a reservation in the name of Jamieson?

PAT:

We might—with certain reservations.

JAMIE:

Can't you possibly rid yourself of them?

PAT:

Did you telegraph?

JAMIE:

I thought I did.

PAT:

How long ago?

JAMIE:

Hours, days, months!

PAT:

That's strange. We don't seem to have any record of—

> JAMIE'S *hand descends upon the piano.*

JAMIE:

Have you room for us or have you not?

PAT:

But we understood it was only for a Single. Who is the party with you?

JAMIE:

My husband.

PAT:

That's what *you* say.

JAMIE:

All right: he's my gentleman-friend. It's—it's just for fun.

PAT:

That's better. Honesty is the best policy.

JAMIE:

Maybe—and maybe not.

PAT:

But chiefly maybe.—You're sure that's all it's for?

JAMIE:

Of course—what else?—Have you one large enough for two, by any chance?

PAT:

Well—we do seem to have something on the second floor. Rather old-fashioned.—Do you mind?

JAMIE:

On the continent.

PAT:

Will the gentleman register?

JAMIE:

I *think* he can sign his name.

> *She moves around him from the piano to-*
> *ward the Hall.*

So you will send up the luggage in a—in a little while?

PAT:

In a very little while, Madam.

JAMIE:

Thank you so very much.

PAT:

Not at all. We look forward to having you with us.

> JAMIE *goes out, without once looking*
> *back.* PAT *smiles and continues to play*
> *softly.*

Curtain

WITHOUT LOVE

ACT III

ACT III

SCENE 1

*It is about half-past seven on an evening in
early October, the same year. The lamps
are lighted and the heavy curtains are
pulled across the windows and the doors
to the terrace. There are red and white
roses in the vases.*

MARTHA, *who is in an evening dress, stands
facing* KITTY, *who is not. There is a moment's silence, then* MARTHA *speaks.*

MARTHA:

So I'm not to concern myself—

KITTY:

Not over me. You might a bit over yourself, if you
like.

MARTHA:

And just what does that mean?

KITTY:

Quent expected you back by Labor Day at the
latest. You didn't come. Then he expected you the
week after. It wasn't until three days ago you arrived.

MARTHA:

My lease on the cottage ran till the First.

147

KITTY:

—And the weather continued fair: sure.

MARTHA:

So therefore he turned to you.

KITTY:

So therefore in the last week or two there've been occasional lunches, dinner and such.

MARTHA:

And such?

KITTY:

I'm sorry: I never fall for heavily veiled implications. You'll have to explain yourself.

> JAMIE, *in a dinner dress, comes in from the Hall and moves swiftly in the direction of the Library.*

JAMIE:

It's late. Is Pat in here, Kitty?

KITTY:

No. He's not back yet.

> JAMIE *slows and stops.*

JAMIE:

It's late. I hope he hurries.

> *To* KITTY.

Oughtn't you to be changing for dinner? I told everyone Eight—and they are prompt, you know.

KITTY:

I sent my little bag up to your dressing room. Was that all right?

148

JAMIE:

But of course. I intended you should. I'm seating you next to Quentin—do you mind?

KITTY:

Not at all.

MARTHA:

Or you might save a chair and just put her in his lap.

JAMIE:

You know, that's quite funny—vulgar, of course, but funny.

MARTHA:

Just tell me how you'd feel if Pat—if some wretched little tartish creature like this started in to—

> KITTY *wheels about suddenly.* MARTHA *stops. There is a moment's silence, then* JAMIE *speaks quietly.*

JAMIE:

Take it back, Martha.

MARTHA:

Why? It's what she is!

> JAMIE *gazes at her for a moment, then turns to* KITTY.

JAMIE:

She's yours, Kitty. Go ahead.

> KITTY *advances a step or two, then stops and turns away.*

But surely you aren't going to let her—?

> KITTY *speaks in a small voice.*

KITTY:

It's all right.

JAMIE:

Not with me, it isn't. Not to a friend of mine in my own house, by Gum!

To MARTHA.

Do you take it back, or don't you?

MARTHA:

Why should I? Who's to make me?

JAMIE:

Yourself, I should hope.

MARTHA:

After a moment.

Well, what do you want me to say?

JAMIE:

"I'm sorry" will be enough.

MARTHA *hesitates, then turns to* KITTY.

MARTHA:

I'm sorry.

KITTY:

It's all right.

MARTHA:

Only look here, Jamie—

JAMIE:

No, my dear—you do! This is Pat's birthday, though he doesn't know I know it. Things haven't been going as they should for him, here lately. I've planned this little dinner for him tonight in the hope of getting his spirits up again.—And by Gum, nobody or nothing's going to spoil it, if I can help it.

MARTHA:

Of course, if you put it that way—

JAMIE:

That's the way I put it! So you'll either behave, or you can just have a saucer of cream in the pantry.

MARTHA:

I think I'd like a cocktail right now, if I may.

JAMIE:

I ordered them served in the little room. Would you mind asking there?

> MARTHA *moves toward the Hall.*

MARTHA:

Don't worry about me this evening. I'll be charming.

> *She goes out.* JAMIE *gazes after her.*

KITTY:

Thanks very much.

JAMIE:

Suspicion—jealousy—possessiveness—oh, if ever I show so much as a sign of them—!

KITTY:

You aren't likely to, are you?

JAMIE:

Watch me tonight, Kitty.

KITTY:

What for?

JAMIE:

She's coming.

KITTY:

She?

JAMIE:

His once-on-a-time—a ghost from his past—his heartbreak—his Lila. And in a white dress, I'll bet, with a top-knot of curls, saying "What, darling? What, sweet?"

KITTY:

Lila Hattersfield?

JAMIE:

Born Lila Vine.—It's an awful name, don't you think?

KITTY:

Yes, it's a pip, all right.

JAMIE:

I hate her.

KITTY laughs.

I'd just like to give him a real dose of her, some-time.

KITTY:

Jamie, you fool—you know he won't even stay in the same room with her! At the Welleses that day, he—

JAMIE:

Yes: I saw. He knew it was her own lovely back halfway across the room—and won't go anywhere since, that she's likely to be.

KITTY:

Then why, for Pete's sake, invite her to dinner?

JAMIE:

I didn't. She's staying with the Hoods now, and they asked could she come. Pat doesn't know yet. I'm sure she put them up to it.

KITTY:

Why can't women like that stay home of an evening?

JAMIE:

What I couldn't make out, was why *you* took what you did so meekly from Martha.

KITTY:

I—I just didn't want to get Quent into any more hot water. He has a tough enough time as it is and—you know—he's so gentle, really, and—and so easily hurt. So I thought if well, if *he* can take the beatings he does—well, I—I just thought it was better to—you know—to let it go.

JAMIE:

Why, Kitty Trimble!

KITTY:

What?

JAMIE *shakes her head over her.*

JAMIE:

Kitty, Kitty, Kitty—

KITTY:

Why? What's the—?

JAMIE:

—And I thought you were proof against anything.
> KITTY *laughs nervously.*

KITTY:

Honestly, Jamie, when you get cryptic—

JAMIE:

And of all people, Quent Ladd—

KITTY:

> *Suddenly, savagely.*

And I love him! I love the great oaf! What do you want to make of it?

JAMIE:

What would I? *She* doesn't. I think it's wonderful.

KITTY:

Like fun, it is! I told her the truth: he doesn't love me a bit—not one bit.

JAMIE:

Maybe not yet, but—

KITTY:

No. Never. All he wants is to sleep with me.—And he just can't understand why I won't.

JAMIE:

But I thought it was all right to, so long as you loved them.—Oh dear—maybe I've been wrong again.

KITTY:

What's worrying you, Jamie?

JAMIE:

Kitty—can you keep a secret?

154

KITTY:

I never have yet, but I'll try.

JAMIE:

Hard?

KITTY:

Terribly.

JAMIE:

We're in the same boat. I'm in love, too. I'm up to my ears in it.

KITTY:

Who with? Paul Carrel again?

JAMIE:

Heavens, no—and never was. That was just the Quentin in me.

KITTY:

All right: I give up.

JAMIE:

It's Pat.

> KITTY *laughs.*

KITTY:

Why, you shameless hussy—and him with a wife!

JAMIE:

You don't understand. We made a solemn pact not to. We both swore we'd never.—But all the same I woke up one morning, and there I was—in love.

KITTY:

And he wasn't?

> JAMIE *shakes her head again, solemnly.*

JAMIE:

I thought maybe he would be—but no. He was just awfully gay and frisky and I could tell I'd been just a—a lark to him: another girl—a gay girl. And that's all I've been since.

KITTY:

He doesn't know?

JAMIE:

—But I live in terror that he will!

KITTY:

But, darling—surely sooner or later he'll—

JAMIE:

No. You don't know him: he'd run a mile. He told me before we married that if ever again he saw the slightest sign of it in himself or anyone else, he'd show her the cleanest pair of heels a girl ever saw.

KITTY:

That's what they are all right—the two of them.

JAMIE:

Who? What?

KITTY:

Quentin and him—a very clean pair of heels.

Suddenly JAMIE *clings to her.*

JAMIE:

Oh, Kitty—let's insult them some more!

KITTY:

The rats.

JAMIE:

The pigs.

156

KITTY:

The—the low-down—
Words fail her.

JAMIE:

—Snakes!

KITTY:

Long Island Lothario.

JAMIE:

Elgin, Illinois Lochinvar. Who do they think they are?

KITTY:

Search me.

JAMIE *moves from her.*

JAMIE:

But he's an angel really. We get on magically. People are forever saying, "What a happy marriage"—damn them!—Oh, Kitty, you don't know what it's like to have been half-dead for years and then suddenly come to life again. Half the time I feel light as air, sort of swinging from limb to limb like Tarzan—and the other half I'm sunk in woe, so terrified of losing him I nearly run away myself.

KITTY:

Mightn't be such a bad idea for awhile.

JAMIE:

I don't believe the man ever lived whose—whose personal freedom meant more to him. He kept his part of the bargain—oh, why couldn't I keep mine?

157

KITTY:

If you made one against love when you married, you flew straight in the face of the Fates, you know.

JAMIE's *head sinks.*

JAMIE:

I know we did. I know it now, all right. I—I just hope I can take my punishment.

KITTY:

Oh, my dear—I was joking, really.

JAMIE:

I'm not. I can't any more. The minute it hit me every grain of humor left me. I can be gay—I can sparkle sort of wetly when I try hard—but all I've got left of what we started with together, is honesty and courage, so I've had to double up on those.

KITTY:

That might be what's changed you, Jamie. You have changed, you know.

JAMIE:

So has he. He's got so jumpy and—and so far away —so distant. Maybe even though he doesn't know it, my being this way irks him somehow.

KITTY:

Now don't you start that!

JAMIE:

Or maybe it's because *she's* around—you know— emanating.

KITTY:

Nonsense. He's just upset and nervous because he

hasn't yet been able to straddle the Irish Channel.

EMMET *comes in from the Hall, rosy in dinner clothes.*

Speaking of which—

JAMIE:

Emmet!

EMMET:

I hope I'm in the right place?

JAMIE:

Quick—tell me! Have they arrived?

EMMET:

My credentials?—At the Legation this morning.

He taps his breast-pocket.

—On my own person now.

JAMIE:

What do they make you? Something really important?

EMMET *draws himself up.*

EMMET:

In the future you may address me as Mr. Special Envoy-at-large for Irish Home Defense, Pro Tem.

KITTY:

Or just "Sugar," for short.

She gathers up her papers and goes out into the Library.

EMMET:

—But let no one forget the "Pro Tem." I like the ring of the Latin.

JAMIE:

An official Irishman with an open mind! Pat will be simply—he doesn't know, does he?

EMMET:

But I shall be happy to grant him my first audience.

JAMIE:

Birthdays are the thing!

EMMET:

It's good to feel of consequence again. It restores the bounce to a man.

> As PAT *comes in, also in dinner clothes,*
> EMMET *bounces himself down full length*
> *upon the sofa.*

I'm the walkin' Playboy of the Western World, who killed his Da with a single clout.

PAT:

Get him up from there and get him to bed.

> EMMET *sits up, aggrieved.*

EMMET:

I've not had a drop since the morning!

PAT:

Then that's what's the matter.

JAMIE:

How did it go, Pat?

PAT:

At the Department of Static?—So far, no farther. God, what a place—not just red-tape—red adhesive

160

tape. Make mine a hemlock and soda, will you?

EMMET *rises and faces him with dignity.*

EMMET:

Young man, you may address me now, if you will.

PAT:

Hello, old boy. How are you?

EMMET:

No such familiarity, if you please.

*He draws a long envelope from his pocket
and flourishes it at him.*

Rest your eyes upon who it is that you're talking
to.

PAT *reads the designation on the envelope.*

PAT:

Since when?

EMMET:

This forenoon.

PAT:

Then what have you been doing all day?

EMMET:

What is it I should have been?

PAT:

Just waiting for your Destiny, I suppose—and missing it, like the rest of your countrymen.

EMMET:

Pleased.

The poet Yeats said that of us—said it was remark-
able, how we always could. Well—we're a remark-
able people.

PAT:

The Germans think so. Berlin's getting more out of Dublin than weather reports.

EMMET:

To JAMIE.

Now he's turning ugly.

PAT:

Wait till we really turn.

JAMIE:

Pat—I think he's ready to help now.

PAT:

To EMMET.

All right—what'll you give for an end to the Partition—guaranteed by us?

EMMET:

We'll make no bargains. Whoever arrives in those Ports unasked, will find the water very hot in them.

PAT:

You see? It's hopeless any way you come at it.

JAMIE:

No! No—it's not!

PAT:

Again to EMMET.

All right: We've been preparing bases in Ulster, as you know. Suppose we moved a few troops in *there* —a division or two, say—what would you feel about that in the Free State?

EMMET:

We'd never allow it—and you wouldn't dare.

162

PAT:

My guess would be, first resentment, then envy. Of course, I'm all balled up at the moment, but that would be my guess.

> *He rises abruptly.*

Do you know what it will cost us to go around the North? Eight to ten millions a day—and God knows how many ships and men in that sweet submarine area.—All right—around we'll go if we must—but don't look even for crumbs at the Peace Table.

EMMET:

Threats, is it?

PAT:

It could be put that way.—Though we'll keep it open for some time, of course, still being slightly soft-headed about you.

EMMET:

I cannot yet speak in officio. I'm too new at it.

PAT:

Then learn—and quick! Or else get ready, the lot of you, for the fate that's reserved for cowards and grudge-bearers.

JAMIE:

Pat—

> EMMET *confronts him.*

EMMET:

That I cannot allow to be said!

JAMIE:

Really, Pat—

PAT:

I withdraw the "cowards." It's true they're never that.

> *To* EMMET.

I'll substitute "blockheads"—is that all right with you?

> *Then he really explodes.*

Holy Hat, Emmet! When will you Irish stop acting so British?

EMMET:

I—you—

> *He swallows and clears his throat.*

Where can a man find that wherewith to wet his whistle?

JAMIE:

In the little room. I'll—

PAT:

No, Jamie. Wait a minute.

> EMMET *lowers his head and bears in the direction of the Hall.*

EMMET:

I don't know why it is no one ever complains about Swiss neutrality.

> *He goes out.* PAT *sinks down into his chair again.*

PAT:

—One hell of a mess all around: me and Neville Henderson: the Failure of a Mission.

JAMIE:

Pat—don't mourn. You'll get there somehow.—Anyhow, happy birthday, Pat.

PAT:

How'd you find that out, you sleuth?

JAMIE:

I asked why the bells were ringing.

PAT:

You didn't tell people, I hope?

JAMIE:

I didn't say whose. I just said a little birthday party.

PAT:

That's fine. Then they'll never suspect, will they?
     JAMIE *looks at him.*

JAMIE:

Funny—one of the things I'll be fighting for, when we fight, is the right to be gay on a birthday.

PAT:

Jamie—I'm sunk, I'm off my beam, I'm bushed.

JAMIE:

Don't be, darling. Things will look up, I promise you.

PAT:

But what's the matter with all of us, anyhow? Are we without any real love of country, any real love of liberty, any love whatsoever for—

JAMIE:

It's not always such a good thing to be, is it?

PAT:

What?

JAMIE:

Without love.

PAT:

No. No, it's not. No—not always. Maybe never.
Then after a moment.
—Emmet and who else for dinner?

JAMIE:

Just a few. I hope you'll like them.

PAT:

Who are they?

JAMIE:

Just old friends—and a few surprises.

PAT:

Do I know them?

JAMIE:

All but one.

PAT:

And who might that be?

JAMIE:

Very difficult to obtain—strictly out of season—but
Never Say Die's what did it.

PAT:

Tell me, you wretched girl.

JAMIE:

Grant Vincent!

PAT:

What!

JAMIE:

Himself.

PAT:

How did you do it?

JAMIE:

Just asked prettily.

PAT:

I hope you didn't have to sit up and beg.

JAMIE:

Not quite.—I used to know him quite well, you know.

PAT:

I remember you said—you and your husband.

JAMIE:

Harry, too.—Why? What's the matter?

PAT:

Nothing at all.

JAMIE:

But aren't you glad he's coming?

PAT:

Oh, tremendously! Very sweet of him to consent at last to meet up with a—what is it I am? Oh yes—an Europeanized American.

JAMIE:

Why, you old grudge-bearer, yourself.

PAT:

Sorry.

JAMIE:

I knew that you'd wanted desperately to see

167

him and—and hadn't been able to, so I thought—

PAT:

—It might be accomplished through your own tender offices. Swell: I'm much obliged.

JAMIE:

Of course, you're making me feel simply grand about it.

PAT:

It's a very friendly act on your part, Jamie. I just don't want any of his damned condescension, that's all.

JAMIE:

There won't be any—not possibly. He's nice as can be, when you know him.

He presses her arm and turns away.

PAT:

All my fault. I didn't eat any lunch. I'll improve on nourishment. Thanks ever so much, honest and true. If your other two surprises are as nice—

QUENTIN *comes in from the Hall in the blue uniform of a Lieutenant of Naval Aviation, but without Wings.*

QUENTIN:

Hello, kids.

PAT:

What splendid sight is this?

QUENTIN:

Where's Martha?

168

JAMIE:

She and Mr. Riordan are in the little room having cocktails.

QUENTIN:

A constructive idea. May I join them?

JAMIE:

Do. We'll be in in a minute.

> QUENTIN *finds a cigarette and lights it.*

QUENTIN:

Look, fellows, I'm in a jam.

JAMIE:

Pretty?

PAT:

What type? What coloring?

QUENTIN:

Wrong—it's this desk job of mine. I want to get off my fanny and into active flying service.

PAT:

Well, if old Sleepy Head's waked at last, there may be hope!

QUENTIN:

Can you fix me up, Doctor?

PAT:

I might know those who could.

QUENTIN:

Good. Because God never meant me to be a waffle-bottom.

JAMIE:

What does Martha think of it?

QUENTIN:

She swears she'll really leave me, if I do.

PAT:

Well?

QUENTIN:

That's one of the reasons I'm so serious about it.—
Has Kitty gone home?

PAT:

In the library, finishing up.

   QUENTIN *moves in that direction.*

QUENTIN:

I've just about decided to put my polo fields into
soy beans and my faith in the Democratic Party.

JAMIE:

Quent—

QUENTIN:

Yes, James?

JAMIE:

The little room's in the other direction.

   He stops and turns.

QUENTIN:

More trouble?

JAMIE:

There might be.—You're next her at dinner, anyway.

   QUENTIN *returns to them.*

QUENTIN:

I know. I gave the place-cards a gander, to see what
Protocol was and my luck might be.—Who's this—

er—Mrs. Vine Hattersfield, on my other side?
>PAT *wheels suddenly.*

PAT:

What did you say?

QUENTIN:

—Vine Hattersfield—between you and me. What about her?

>PAT *turns away. There is a moment's silence. Then* JAMIE *speaks:*

JAMIE:

She's an American girl married to a—divorced now, I think. Or at any rate—

QUENTIN:

That's promising. Has she got any looks?

JAMIE:

Quantities, I believe.

>QUENTIN *proceeds toward the Hall.*

QUENTIN:

For safety's sake I'll concentrate on her.

>*And goes out. There is another silence. Then* PAT *speaks quietly.*

PAT:

How did it happen?

JAMIE:

The Hoods asked if they might bring her.

PAT:

You should have said no.

JAMIE:

How could I?

PAT:

Simply by saying it.

JAMIE:

I'm not very good at that sort of thing, Pat.

PAT:

Then it's time you learned. This is one hell of a thing.

JAMIE:

Pat—mind your manners! Naturally, if close friends like the Hoods—

PAT:

I think it was deliberate.

JAMIE:

I'm sure it was. But so far as I'm concerned, I'm rather relieved to know that at last—

PAT:

"At last" what?

JAMIE:

—That the hide-and-seek's over! It's been stupid and humiliating, to say the least, and I've hated it.

PAT:

Hide and seek?

JAMIE:

All summer long—you know you've been going miles out of your way to avoid her. Isn't it quite a situation you're making out of something that ought to be simple—and casual—and over and done with?

PAT:

That's just it—it *is* over and done with. Let it stay that way! This is one hell of an attitude: Do you realize you're objecting, not to my seeing too much of a girl but to my wish not to see her at all?

JAMIE:

To my mind, that's much worse.

PAT:

You're wrong on all counts.

JAMIE:

I don't think so.

PAT:

Sorry. The fact remains that if she comes here to-night, I go out—and in one hell of a hurry.

JAMIE:

Stop saying "one hell of"! You know it's too late now. You must realize—

> *There is a sound in the Hall.* PAT *moves toward the Library.*

PAT:

Good night. See you later.

JAMIE:

Pat!

PAT:

What?

JAMIE:

Don't do this!

PAT:

Sorry—be seeing you—

JAMIE:

You will see me again after you have seen her.

PAT:

That will be quite a while.

JAMIE:

After a moment.

I'll leave that to you. I mean it, Pat. I'll be out and away by morning—no—by tonight. I can't live this way, with anything of this sort between us.

PAT:

"This sort"! What sort?

JAMIE:

I'll go back to where I began—the other side of you —the other side of Harry even: I've got things to find there. You've got things to find, too—and you'll have to settle and solve them yourself.

PAT:

Just as you say.

JAMIE:

—Yes, Pat: just that way.

PETER BAILLIE *and* GRANT VINCENT *come in from the Hall, both in dinner coats.* VINCENT *is about fifty, youthful in appearance and movement, graying slightly, looking like business.* JAMIE *goes to them.*

Peter—Grant! You were sweet to come to my birthday party.

PETER:

Yours? I thought—

JAMIE:

Oh, no—*I'm* the aging one!

VINCENT:

All my best.

JAMIE:

Isn't it a shame my husband can't be here for it?

PETER:

But I see him.

PAT:

Sorry—I'm due somewhere else and in one hell of a—

JAMIE:

—And you're late! You'd better rush. Do you know my husband, Grant?

VINCENT:

How are you?

PAT:

Pretty well, considering. How are you?

VINCENT:

Great.

PAT:

So I've gathered. In fact, the true Unapproachable.
He looks him up and down.

—You hear about these great men, and then you meet them.
He moves toward the Library.

See you again sometime, I hope.

VINCENT:

Any time. When?
        PAT *stops and turns.*

175

PAT:

Well, all I've got free this week is Monday, Tuesday, Wednesday, Thursday, Friday and Saturday.

VINCENT:

How about driving up to Annapolis with me at noon tomorrow?

PAT:

It's a date.

> ANNA *appears in the Hall doorway.*

ANNA:

Sir Richard and Lady Hood, Madam. And Mrs. Hattersfield. Which way shall I—?

JAMIE:

The little room. I'm coming.

> ANNA *goes out,* JAMIE *moving after her.*

VINCENT:

> *Simultaneously to* PAT.

I'll have the car stop for you.

PAT:

Do that.

> *He goes out.*

JAMIE:

Richard? Sylvie? Hello, my dears!

VINCENT:

> *To* PETER.

Independent cuss, isn't he?

PETER:

But a lot on the ball.

> JAMIE *mounts the steps to the Hall.*

JAMIE:

—And Mrs. Hattersfield! What an enchanting dress! That's really one hell of a one, Mrs. Hattersfield.

> *She goes out.* VINCENT *and* PETER *move after her toward the Hall.*

Curtain

ACT III

SCENE 2

It is about half-past ten at night, late November, the same year. Lamps are lighted, curtains are drawn, fireplace is burning, but there is not a flower of any sort anywhere in the room. VINCENT *is at the telephone.* HOOD *is seated and* PAT *stands near him.* VINCENT *alone is in dinner clothes.*

VINCENT:

> *To the telephone.*

I'll wait. I've been waiting all of my life.

HOOD:

Seems a different place with Jamie away, doesn't it?

PAT:

Stay on the subject, Richard.

HOOD:

Spent a week in Maine myself once. Awful place. Nothing but fog. Couldn't see my Bridge-hand before my face.

VINCENT:

—Holding on. But don't do this again.

PAT:

> *To* HOOD.

We had a fling at Empire once or twice, too, you know. And it was pretty dirty business.

178

HOOD:

Can be, old boy! End justifies the means, however. When they can't rule themselves—

PAT:

You don't give them the chance to. You grab and hold on.

HOOD:

Now take India—

VINCENT:

—Can't. *You* took it.

> *Then to the telephone.*

Yes—yes. Certainly! Why not? What type of planes has he in mind?—Oh, for the love of—! Tell him we'll cool 'em with whatever it takes to. We'll use air—water—prestone—we'll use beer, if we have to.

PAT:

What *we're* talking about, is—

HOOD:

—You're not even *in* the war yet.

PAT:

It's coming: you know it is.

HOOD:

So is Christmas.

VINCENT:

> *To the telephone.*

—Is Riordan still with them? Right.—Ask Baillie to call me here directly he leaves. Important. Right.

> *He replaces the telephone and turns.*

Well—what about it?

HOOD:

You've heard Riordan—you've heard De Valera:
you know they won't make a deal.

PAT:

Then don't try to—just *do* it, with no strings at-
tached! They're rewarding, once they find they
can trust you. You might see a whole attitude
changed overnight.

HOOD:

—And might not. Just tell me where we'd be now,
without Ulster—

PAT:

I think you'd have the entire Island behind you.

HOOD:

Yes—right at our back.

VINCENT:

—Something in what Hood says. Look—suppose we
just quietly moved a few ships into those ports and
did the talking afterwards—

HOOD:

Now there's an idea!

PAT:

Take them, you mean?

VINCENT:

In effect.—What would happen?

PAT:

Invasion's invasion. All hell would break loose.

VINCENT:

You think?

PAT:

I know.

VINCENT:

Not worth it?

PAT:

Not at this point. If it comes to that, the other plan's better.

VINCENT:

Troops into the north?

PAT:

And lots of them. At least that's a step, instead of a stumble.

HOOD *looks from one to the other.*

HOOD:

I'll tell you: about the Partition I'll do what I can.

PAT:

That's talking!

HOOD:

—But I know Churchill.

PAT:

Ask him whether or not we all speak the same language. Do we, or do we not?

HOOD:

Well—in a manner of speaking.

PAT:

London English—Dublin English—Sydney, Wellington, Ottawa—Elgin, Illinois English! What the hell!

If *we* can't make sense and get along, what can we do with other languages?

The telephone rings. VINCENT *goes to it.*

VINCENT:

Baillie, I guess.—Yes? Right here. What happened?

A moment. He glances at PAT.

Why yes, a little—naturally. Wouldn't you be, if *your* baby—?

He listens again.

But what did Riordan have to say finally?—I was afraid of that—instructions of course.—What?

A moment. Then he laughs briefly.

Well—that's something!

To PAT.

No go—positively none. But you've made one convert. Your friend says he's going back to join the Honorable Opposition.

PAT *turns away. He speaks lowly:*

PAT:

Yes. It's something.

VINCENT:

To the telephone.

So what's the answer—the other way?—Definitely?—When? Right—but go easy, it's loaded. Yes, I'll tell him.—No—can't—I'm hooked for the Russian Embassy party. Goodbye.

He replaces the telephone and turns to PAT.

Baillie says to cheer up: we often have to go a long way around, to arrive where we're headed for.

PAT:

Troops to Ulster?

VINCENT:

I can't hear you.

Then suddenly, angrily:

Lord—to have to let the Army take this one over, too!

HOOD *rises, now all smiles.*

HOOD:

'Night, Vincent. 'Night, Pat.

VINCENT:

Lunch Monday, Hood. I want to pump you some more.

To PAT.

Now I've *really* got a couple of calls to make.— Use your private phone?

PAT:

It's in here. I'll chase Trimble out.

PAT *goes into the Library.* HOOD *moves toward the Hall.*

HOOD:

—Amazing to me how things get done here this way.

VINCENT:

Dashed irregular, what?

HOOD:

Brother, you have spoken a mouthful.

183

He goes out into the Hall as QUENTIN *comes in, Navy cap in hand, Navy overcoat over arm, Wings on breast.* VINCENT *moves toward the Library.* QUENTIN *calls to him:*

QUENTIN:

Good evening, sir!

KITTY comes in from Library. VINCENT *turns to* QUENTIN.

VINCENT:

You wanted speed: did they come through?

QUENTIN:

My orders? Yes: I'm to leave from Anacostia Field at eleven.

KITTY:

Tonight? Quent!

QUENTIN:

To VINCENT.

I also wanted some real action.

VINCENT:

That's harder to get.—But a little bird tells me you never can tell.

He goes out. QUENTIN *drops his hat and coat on a chair and turns to* KITTY.

QUENTIN:

Will you drive me out to the field?

KITTY:

Come hell or high water.

184

QUENTIN:

I'll miss you, Kid.

KITTY:

What do you think I'll you?

QUENTIN:

Fact?

KITTY:

Hurry home, Quent.

QUENTIN:

When I come back—with a fine tan, but no medals—
I'd like a word with you.

KITTY:

It can be arranged.

QUENTIN:

No soft stuff, mind you—just a practical word or
two.

KITTY:

Oh, eminently.

QUENTIN:

Sure you see what I mean?

KITTY:

No, but I'll work it out.

QUENTIN:

Martha's taken The Step.

KITTY:

Well, I'll be a son of a gun.

QUENTIN:

You've slugged your way right into my heart, you
know.

KITTY:

Can this by any chance be love?

QUENTIN:

Love? Never again! I simply like the hell out of you.

KITTY:

I—return the compliment.

QUENTIN:

Of course, why an absolute first-rater like you should give one thought in the world to a mug like me—

KITTY:

I don't like you humble.

He grins and indicates his uniform.

QUENTIN:

Humble—in this?

KITTY:

Jamie's upstairs dressing. Give her a quick good-bye—then let's go.

QUENTIN:

She's back from Maine?

KITTY:

—And bound for the Russian shindig with Vincent. Pat doesn't know she's back. I'm breaking it to him.

QUENTIN:

You don't think we'd end on the rocks, the way they have?

186

KITTY:

No, Quent, I do not. Nor do I think they have—
yet.

QUENTIN:

One hell of a word—that "yet." Let's throw it out.
He starts toward the Hall. PAT *reenters
from the Library.*

PAT:

Good stuff, Quent.
QUENTIN *goes out.*

QUENTIN:

Maybe!

PAT:

Go whenever you like, Kitty.

KITTY:

Thanks.—Do you want anything?

PAT:

No, thanks.

KITTY:

You didn't eat any dinner.

PAT:

I wanted to see tonight through lean and thirsty.

KITTY:

How did it go?

PAT:

—Right out of my hands: Jamieson to Baillie to
Vincent to Baillie.

KITTY:

That's often the way, here.

PAT:

That was the way.

KITTY:

You started the game though: don't forget that.

PAT:

It's not credit I'm looking for, Kitty. It's action. That we're getting now—of a sort.

KITTY:

Good!

Then, with elaborate casualness:

Oh—er—Jamie's back—or did you know?

PAT:

No, I didn't. Where?

KITTY:

Upstairs.

PAT:

Why?

KITTY:

Chiefly because I telephoned her, I expect.

PAT:

What did you say?

KITTY:

Only that you were lighting out some place to-morrow. I didn't say where, because I didn't know.

PAT:

You're fired.

KITTY:

I wouldn't be surprised.

PAT:

What did *she* say?

KITTY:

She just asked whether two months had been long enough for you to get around to seeing Lila the Hattersfield and I said no, I didn't think so.—And she waited a moment and then said, "Well, he will have by the time he sees me."

PAT:

But he won't.

KITTY:

I think she means you will have.

PAT:

How?

KITTY:

I don't know. Jamie's capable of anything, once her mind's made up. There is the Telegraph, there is the Telephone. The lady may be on the front doorstep now.

PAT:

Doubtful.—Is Jamie really upstairs?

KITTY:

I'll have her tap on the floor, if you like.

PAT:

Don't bother. What else did she say?

KITTY:

Two or three things I didn't get: something about clearing the decks, the Fight for Freedom, and there being too much honesty between husbands and wives.

PAT:

I don't get them either.

KITTY:

Maybe you'd better be prepared for a whopper. Actually, where is it you're off to, and why?

PAT:

None of your business.

KITTY:

I'll bet a hat it's the old self-sacrifice stuff. "I am not good for her. I make her unhappy."

PAT:

You'd lose your hat—also your shirt.

KITTY:

But you've been like a fish out of water without her —you know it. Sure it's not that clean pair of heels you said you'd show, if ever—?

PAT:

"If ever" what—?

KITTY:

Sorry: I go too far.

PAT:

You don't seriously think—er—Lila's coming here, do you?

KITTY:

I wouldn't doubt it for a minute. Give her my best French remembrances, will you? Little Creamy

Face sang her way right into my heart that night.
She certainly loves a party, that girl.

> QUENTIN *comes in from the Hall.*

Ready, Quent?

> QUENTIN *picks up his coat and cap.*

QUENTIN:

Set.—So long again, Pat.

PAT:

Best of everything, boy. You know what I think
of you.

> *They shake hands.*

QUENTIN:

Sweetheart, I'm getting the best—but not how I like
it. I thought at least I'd be ferrying bombers to
England—and I draw that damned lotus-land.

PAT:

They say the girls are something.

> QUENTIN *sings out:*

QUENTIN:

" 'Onika-wiki-wiki,' Sweet Brown Maiden said to
me, as she gave me language lessons on the—"

> *He glances at* KITTY.

Oh—I forgot—I've given all that up. Here we go!

> *He hurries out into the Hall.* KITTY *moves
> swiftly after him.*

KITTY:

Hey! Wait for Baby!

> PAT *starts toward the Library, stops him-
> self, begins to light a cigarette, puts it out,*

then turns and moves slowly to the piano, where he seats himself. He begins to play softly. JAMIE *comes down the steps from the Hall, bright in a white evening-dress. Her hair is worn high and curls, held by a comb, are a crowning-touch to the crowning glory. A pin holds two white orchids at her shoulder and she wears an old-fashioned necklace—white gloves,—anything to complete the perfect picture of the woman of the world who knows her own style and has taken infinite pains to project it. Her voice and her manner are at one with her appearance: she speaks musically and self-assuredly from several neat shelves in her mind, the heart having been left on the dressing-table.*

JAMIE:

Darling! How ever are you?

PAT:

In rude health, thanks. Welcome to Washington. How's yourself?

JAMIE:

I'm simply supreme. Very ept and ert. I gained four pounds then lost them again and I'm full of all sorts and descriptions of mischief. Isn't this fun?

PAT:

What?

JAMIE:

—Your poor frazzled self. You've been working too hard again. It's got to stop.—The North Wind doth blow, and we shall have snow—and what will Poor Patrick do then, poor thing?

> *She seats herself on the edge of the table and sits there, swinging her legs, smiling at him.*

Well? How do I look to you?

PAT:

Slightly over-lighted.

JAMIE:

Just the intention!—Come and kiss me, Sweet-and-Twenty. Youth's a stuff will not endure.

PAT:

Have you been knocking a few off, or something?

JAMIE:

What, darling?—Oh no—just sheer, wonderful, animal spirits!—I love animals, don't you? I love their spirits.—Don't I get a kiss?

PAT:

I don't know what's to prevent.

JAMIE:

It's been ages since we've ever so much as met, hasn't it?

PAT:

Any amount of them.

> JAMIE *holds her arms out to him.*

193

JAMIE:

Darling—

> *He advances. She laughs and drops her arms.*

—But on second thought, no.—I've spent hours on my makeup, and I shouldn't like to disappoint the Russians.

> *A moment. Then:*

What, darling?

PAT:

I didn't say anything.

JAMIE:

What, sweet?

PAT:

I say it'd be a great pity to disappoint the Russians.

> *She laughs merrily.*

JAMIE:

Still the same old Pat: Comes right back at a girl!

PAT:

Let that be my epitaph.

JAMIE:

New York was super. I meant to spend not more than two days on the way down—but I ran into people and what with this and with that, all at once it was five.

PAT:

Shocking.

194

JAMIE:

What, darling?—No, hardly that—just a little innocent fun. Life's been on the dull side. What really lured me from Maine was Litvinov's card and the thought of caviar and champagne and O-chichorn-ia.

PAT:

Crack a bottle of vodka for me.

JAMIE:

You definitely won't come?

PAT:

—Must plead pressure of work, etcetera.

JAMIE:

I was afraid of that. That's why I wired Grant Vincent to squire me. He accepted, with flowers.

She touches her orchids.

Look—aren't they sweet?

PAT:

Right from the White House greenhouse, probably.

Again JAMIE *laughs, lets herself down from the table and moves away from him.*

JAMIE:

—Snitched them from the White House greenhouse. Wear them with the fur-side outside. Wear them with the skin-side inside. Daughter of the Wind, Nokomis.

A moment. Then she turns innocently.

What, darling?

PAT:

I didn't say a word.

She goes to him.

JAMIE:

I'm in an absolute whirr of anticipation. Will you be up when I get home?

PAT:

I doubt it. Why?

JAMIE:

I just thought we might—you know—share a few bedtime confidences?

PAT:

Sorry. I expect to turn in early.

JAMIE:

What's keeping you up, darling?

PAT:

There've been fairly serious things going on here this evening.

JAMIE:

Really? What a bore.

She moves toward the piano.

PAT:

In fact, from the point of view of—

JAMIE:

—Don't tell me.

She seats herself at the piano.

PAT:

No?

196

JAMIE:

No. I'm not in the mood for politics.

PAT:

Who the hell are you, anyway?

JAMIE:

Me?—Me, Jamie Co-Co—Me, French gel. I 'ave brush up on my music *un petit peu*—want to hear?

> *She begins to play and sing a crooning French song in the manner of Lucienne Boyer, somewhat exaggerated.* PAT *stares at her for a moment, then slowly approaches her. Before the song is ended, in a suddenly accelerated movement he is at her side, crushing her hands down with a bang upon the keys.*

PAT:

Now I know what you're up to, you snake-in-the grass!

> JAMIE *rises and moves away from the piano.*

JAMIE:

I thought that's the way you liked them: April in Paris.

PAT:

Oh, you did, did you?

JAMIE:

Yes. I was led to suppose—

PAT:

Oh, you were, were you?—What about Peach—
Cherry—Plum-Blossom Time in Virginia?

JAMIE:

I don't follow you.

PAT:

Oh, you don't, don't you?

JAMIE:

Stop repeating yourself! What I mean to say, is—

PAT:

Keep your voice down. Vincent's telephoning in
there.

He continues to move up on her.

JAMIE:

Wha—what's the idea of this?

PAT:

I'll show you what's the idea.—All that's all over.
It's War-Time in Washington: *that's* the idea!

She retreats. He follows.

JAMIE:

Well, suppose it is? What do you think you're
going to do?

PAT:

I'll show you what I'm going to do.

She puts a table between them.

JAMIE:

Pat, this is idiotic. What are you—?

PAT:

Creamy Little Face, I'm going to cream you.

JAMIE:

Just because I—?

> *Again he follows her. She escapes, leans against the other side of a sofa, panting.*

PAT:

—Because I don't like you this way. I don't like your looks. I don't like your manner. I don't like the way you wear your hair. That's what chiefly annoys me.—Look at yourself, turnip-top!

> *Involuntarily she turns to the mirror. He leaps up on the sofa above her, bends and grasps the top-knot.*

JAMIE:

Stop it, you beastly—! By Gum, what do you think you're doing?

> *He dangles the three false curls on their pin.*

PAT:

God! Not even your own!

JAMIE:

They are too, mine! They were in a box in my father's desk down in Maine.

PAT:

Were you in Maine at all?

JAMIE:

Certainly I was in Maine. What makes you think—

PAT:

I just thought you might be lying.

JAMIE:

I don't lie.

PAT:

Oh, no—not you!

> *She combs her hair out before the mirror, her back to him.*

JAMIE:

And where is it you think you're off to in the morning? Kitty said—. You might have written me once or twice.

PAT:

—You might have written me, but after all, why? We were too much out of step.

JAMIE:

We were out of step all right. We've been an odd pair, in our separate ways, haven't we?

PAT:

Those separate ways: perhaps we ought to mend them.

JAMIE:

Those separate ways—I thought we'd just wend them.

> *Now he is watching her more and more intently.*

PAT:

Did you really?

JAMIE:

Well, it—it just didn't work out, did it?

PAT:

Not as we planned—nope—would seem not.

JAMIE:

We'd no right to expect it to, I expect.

PAT:

Noble experiment, anyhow.

JAMIE:

Funny, how important that missing element really is.

PAT:

Live and learn!

JAMIE:

Nothing quite takes its place ever, I guess.

PAT:

Not in a month of Sundays.

JAMIE:

With it, anything's possible, however hard to bear. But without—

She falls silent a moment. Then, brightly:

—And now with your beautiful freedom back again! I wonder what you'll be doing with it—

PAT:

Remembering your shining face, I expect.

JAMIE:

That's sweet, Pat. It's very sweet. I think I'll settle for that.

She moves from him. He advances.

PAT:

Jamie! I'll tell you where I'm going: three days ago, I—

He stops as VINCENT *reenters from the Library.*

VINCENT:

How are you, Jamie?

JAMIE:

He-hello, Grant.

VINCENT:

Your young man's balled things up quite successfully in your absence.

JAMIE:

I—I'm so glad.

VINCENT:

> *To* PAT.

I've just been on the phone with the Boss about it. He's most appreciative. Says however it's come out, it was you who started the ball rolling and kept it rolling.

> *He looks at him slyly.*

—Wonders what you personally expect to get out of it.

PAT:

Tell him not to get me sore. I might mutiny.

VINCENT:

Not the privilege of civilians.

PAT:

Maybe that's what I was thinking of, when I enlisted.

VINCENT:

When you what?

JAMIE:

Pat!

PAT:

—Enlisted, I said.

VINCENT:

As what?

PAT:

Apprentice seaman.

JAMIE:

Oh, Pat!

VINCENT:

But we meant to send him to Ireland with Riordan!

PAT:

Me?

VINCENT:

—As Special Attaché—next week—and none more welcome, *he* said: "The swans on the Liffey will bend their proud necks to him."

>   *To* JAMIE.

Just two or three months or so.—Would you mind? Just to ease certain news to them all.

JAMIE:

How could I? What rights has a sailor's wife?

PAT:

—But I'm in the Navy and I'm going to Norfolk tomorrow!

VINCENT:

You'll go where you're ordered, you low-down gob.

WITHOUT LOVE

> *To* JAMIE.

Are you sure you want to go to the Russians this evening?

JAMIE:

I was. Now I'm not so.

VINCENT:

> *To* PAT.

You've got six days. Get out of town—get some rest. You're a great pair. Love is indeed wonderful.

> JAMIE *and* PAT *exchange glances, then begin to speak with mounting vehemence.*

JAMIE:

But the one thing we're not, is in love.

PAT:

And never expect to be.

JAMIE:

Don't want it!

PAT:

Wouldn't have it around.

JAMIE:

Not if we live to be a hundred, by Gum!

PAT:

We just get along, that's all.

JAMIE:

—At least part of the time.

PAT:

So is that understood?

VINCENT:

—All I wish is that I could find someone who didn't

love me, the way you two don't each other. *He goes out into the Hall.* PAT *takes an envelope from his pocket and moves toward the fireplace with it.* JAMIE *follows.*

JAMIE:

What's that?

PAT:

A note I was going to leave for you.

JAMIE:

Give it to me—it's mine!

> PAT *tears it in two and throws it into the fireplace.*

PAT:

Contents already noted.

> *A moment, then she slips her arm through his.*

JAMIE:

Oh, Pat—I hope you'll be snug and warm in your little sailor suit.

PAT:

Let's not think of any of that for six days.

JAMIE:

Six whole days!

> *Together they start to move toward the Hall.*

Where will we spend them?

PAT:

We'll plan something, darling.

JAMIE:

Hot Springs is cold in December.

PAT:

There are other places not so. What's wrong with this?

JAMIE:

Nothing, Pat—oh, not a thing! Wait: we're still out of—

She falls into step with him.

—There!

PAT:

Now are we in?

JAMIE:

By Gum, if we're not, I don't know who is!

They go out.

Curtain

Location of call numbers in
CENTRAL LIBRARY

A	E	J	In
B	F	K	CIRCULATION
C	G	L	ROOM
D	H	P	
	HM-HX		

HA-HJ			In
Q	T		SCIENCE AND
R	U		INDUSTRY ROOM
S	V		

M			In
N			ART AND MUSIC
			ROOM

REFERENCE or **REFERENCE ROOM** above call number: book to be used in library only.

"j" before the call number: book is in CHILDREN'S ROOM.

' before the call number: refers to loca- of book in the Room housing that call

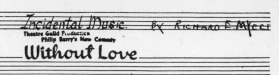

1

Incidental Music. By Richard E. Myers

Theatre Guild Production
Philip Barry's New Comedy

Without Love

ACT I · SCENE II ·

THEME SONG 1

(Warning) CURTAIN ACT I. SCENE I. "QUENTIN, TELL ME ONE OF YOUR FUNNY STORIES. I WANT TO LAUGH".

(Cue) ABOUT 30 SECONDS AFTER FALL OF CURTAIN PLAY THEME SONG TO ITS FINISH.

Tempo di Valse.

MODERATO—

SOFTER AT CURTAIN—

·3·

The Theatre Guild Presents
Philip Barry's New Comedy
Without Love

THEME SONG 2

ACT II · SCENE II. (A)

Warning: "GOD LOVE YOU"

Cue: AT SIGNAL PLAY LOUDLY AND IN OCTAVES TO ~~FINISH~~ FIRST NOTE OF 13th BAR.
END ON ABRUPT CHORD.

Tempo di Valse

(f) Quickly —

STOP

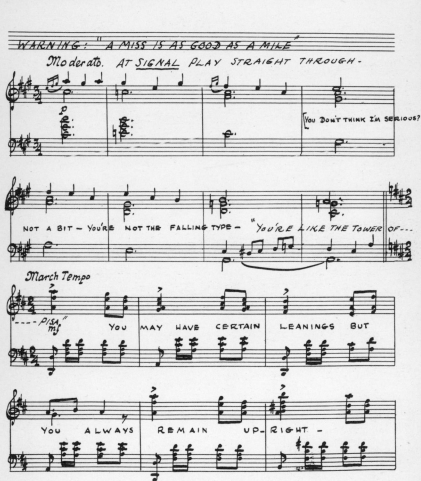

Without Love. Ear phones—

Act II · Scene II (B)   Richard E. Myers

Scene v. Jamie & Pat.

WARNING: "A MISS IS AS GOOD AS A MILE"

Moderato. AT SIGNAL PLAY STRAIGHT THROUGH—

You Don't think I'm serious?

NOT A BIT — You're NOT THE FALLING TYPE — "You're LIKE THE TOWER OF —

March Tempo

—— PISA," YOU MAY HAVE CERTAIN LEANINGS BUT

YOU ALWAYS REMAIN UP-RIGHT —

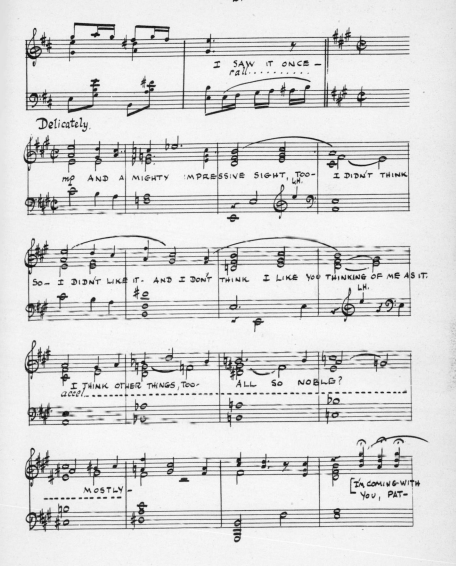

VERY — A CHARMING PLACE YOU HAVE HERE — SELDOM

A COMPLAINT —

[HAVE YOU A RESERVATION
IN THE NAME OF JAMIESON—]?

WARNING: "WE MIGHT WITH CERTAIN RESERVATIONS" CUE: CAN'T YOU POSSIBLY RID YOURSELF ---
rit --------- rit.

Come in a "rid yourself of 'them'"

THEME SONG. Tempo di Valse

--- OF THEM" DID YOU TELEGRAPH? I THOUGHT I DID— HOW LONG AGO?

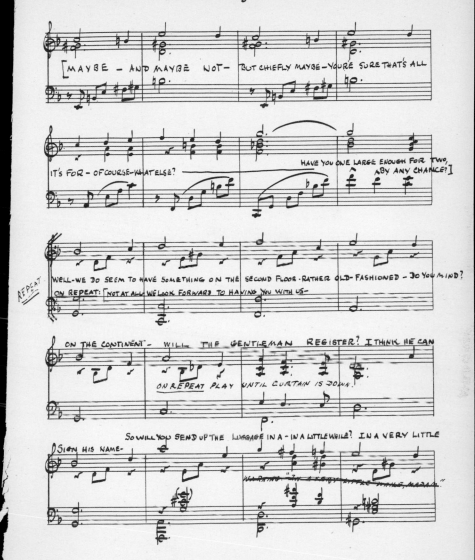

WHILE, MADAM.   GUE: THANK YOU SO VERY MUCH.   PLAY ARPEGGIO IN F AND GO BACK TO REPEAT AGAIN.   REPEAT.

morendo . . . .   ppp

ppp.

THEME SONG ③